LEOPARD TORTOISE

A Thorough Guide On Leopard Tortoise Care Guide: Feeding, Health Care, Habitat, Breeding And Choosing The Right Species As Pets

Pet Leonard

Table of Contents

Introduction to Leopard Tortoises as Pets

Leopard tortoises (*Stigmochelys pardalis*) are one of the most popular choices for reptile enthusiasts due to their striking shell patterns, gentle nature, and manageable size compared to other tortoise species. Native to the savannas and grasslands of Africa, they are named for the unique, spotted patterns on their shells, reminiscent of a leopard's coat. These tortoises are herbivorous, hardy, and relatively easy to care for with the proper knowledge and preparation, making them an attractive choice for both beginner and experienced reptile keepers.

However, owning a leopard tortoise is a long-term commitment, as they can live up to 50 years or more with proper care. They are also a species that requires specific environmental conditions, including temperature, humidity, and diet, to thrive. Understanding their natural habits and needs is critical to providing them with a happy, healthy life in captivity.

Understanding the Leopard Tortoise

The leopard tortoise is the fourth largest tortoise species in the world, with adults typically weighing between 20 and 50 pounds and reaching lengths of 10 to 18 inches. They are native to a broad range of habitats across sub-Saharan Africa, including dry savannas, scrublands, and semi-arid regions. Their adaptability in the wild allows them to thrive in diverse environments, but replicating these conditions in captivity is key to their well-being.

Physical Characteristics

The leopard tortoise is easily identifiable by its high-domed shell adorned with yellow and black spots or blotches. This pattern not only gives them their name but also helps them blend into their natural environment. Their limbs are strong and sturdy, allowing them to traverse rugged terrain. Unlike some tortoise species, leopard tortoises lack a hinged shell and cannot completely withdraw their heads and limbs for protection.

Behavior and Temperament

Leopard tortoises are generally calm and docile, which makes them ideal for pet owners who prefer low-maintenance and non-aggressive pets. While not particularly social, they can become accustomed to human presence and may even recognize their owners over time, especially during feeding. They are diurnal, meaning they are active during the day, and spend most of their time grazing on grasses or basking in the sun.

Why Choose a Leopard Tortoise as a Pet?

Owning a leopard tortoise offers several benefits for those interested in unique and exotic pets. Here are some compelling reasons to choose a leopard tortoise:

Stunning Appearance

The leopard-like spots and intricate shell patterns make them one of the most visually striking tortoise species. Their elegant design adds an aesthetic appeal that draws many pet owners to them.

Docile Nature

Leopard tortoises are known for their calm demeanor. They rarely exhibit aggression and are easy to handle, making them suitable for families and individuals alike.

Long Lifespan

While their long lifespan requires a significant commitment, it also allows for a lifelong bond. Unlike other pets with shorter lifespans, a leopard tortoise can remain a part of your family for decades.

Low Noise and Odor

Unlike dogs or cats, leopard tortoises are incredibly quiet and produce minimal odor when their habitat is properly maintained. This makes them ideal for households with noise restrictions or individuals seeking a peaceful pet.

Educational and Interactive Experience

Owning a leopard tortoise offers a unique opportunity to learn about reptile care, ecosystems, and conservation. Watching their behaviors and understanding their needs can be both educational and rewarding.

Minimal Space Requirements

While they do need an appropriately sized enclosure, leopard tortoises do not require the constant attention or roaming space that some larger pets, like dogs, need. This makes them suitable for homes with limited outdoor or indoor space.

Considerations Before Owning a Leopard Tortoise

While leopard tortoises have many attractive qualities, potential owners must also consider the responsibilities involved:

Specialized Care: They require a controlled habitat with specific temperature, humidity, and UV lighting conditions.

Long-Term Commitment: Their long lifespan means they may outlive their owners, so long-term planning is essential.

Legal Regulations: Some regions have restrictions on owning or importing leopard tortoises, so it's important to check local laws.

Initial Costs: Setting up a proper enclosure and providing for their dietary and health needs can be costly.

By thoroughly researching and preparing, leopard tortoise owners can enjoy the unique experience of caring for this incredible species while ensuring their pet lives a healthy and fulfilling life.

Chapter One

Natural Habitat and Behavior of Leopard Tortoises

Leopard tortoises (*Stigmochelys pardalis*) are fascinating reptiles native to the African continent. Their adaptability and resilience allow them to thrive in diverse environments, but understanding their origin and distribution is crucial for providing appropriate care in captivity.

Origin and Distribution

Geographical Range

Leopard tortoises are indigenous to sub-Saharan Africa and are widely distributed across a range of countries, including:

Southern Africa: South Africa, Botswana, Namibia, and Zimbabwe.

Eastern Africa: Kenya, Tanzania, and Uganda.

Western and Central Africa: Chad, Nigeria, and Sudan.

Their wide distribution showcases their ability to adapt to various climates and terrains. However, they are predominantly found in regions with semi-arid and grassland ecosystems.

Natural Habitats

Leopard tortoises inhabit diverse environments, including:

- **Savannas**: These open grasslands are their primary habitat. The abundance of grasses and shrubs provides ample food sources, while the warm climate aligns with their ectothermic (cold-blooded) nature.
- **Scrublands**: These areas are characterized by sparse vegetation and sandy soils, which leopard tortoises navigate with ease due to their sturdy legs.
- **Semi-Arid Regions**: While these areas can be harsh, leopard tortoises are well-adapted to survive in such environments, relying on hardy vegetation and their ability to conserve water.

They tend to avoid dense forests and extremely dry deserts, as these areas do not provide suitable conditions for grazing or maintaining their body temperature.

Climate Preferences

Leopard tortoises thrive in warm climates with plenty of sunlight. Their natural habitat typically features:

Temperature: Daytime temperatures range from 75°F to 95°F (24°C to 35°C), with cooler nights. They are intolerant of prolonged cold temperatures and require warmth to maintain their metabolism.

Rainfall: While they are adapted to arid regions, seasonal rains play a vital role in their habitat. Rain encourages the growth of fresh grasses and provides drinking water.

In captivity, replicating these conditions is essential for their health. Owners must provide a warm environment with proper lighting and humidity levels to mimic their native habitat.

Behavior in the Wild

Leopard tortoises exhibit unique behaviors that help them survive and thrive in their natural environment:

Grazing and Feeding

As herbivores, leopard tortoises primarily graze on grasses, leaves, and succulents. Their strong, beak-like jaws allow them to tear through tough vegetation. They are also known to consume calcium-rich sources like bones or snail shells to support their shell development.

Basking

Leopard tortoises are diurnal, meaning they are active

during the day. They spend a significant amount of time basking in the sun to regulate their body temperature. Early mornings and late afternoons are their most active times, as midday heat can be intense.

Water Conservation

In their arid habitats, water can be scarce. Leopard tortoises are highly efficient at conserving water and can go long periods without drinking. They often obtain moisture from dew, succulent plants, and seasonal rain.

Burrowing and Shelter

While they do not burrow as extensively as some tortoise species, leopard tortoises seek shelter under bushes, rocks, or in natural crevices to escape extreme heat or predators.

Mating and Reproduction

During the rainy season, leopard tortoises become more active, and this is also their primary mating period. Males will court females by circling them and engaging in vocalizations. Females lay eggs in burrows, which they dig in sandy soil. Hatchlings are highly vulnerable to predators and rely on their camouflage for survival.

Conservation Status

Leopard tortoises are not currently classified as endangered, but their populations face threats from habitat destruction, agricultural expansion, and the illegal pet trade. Conservation efforts focus on habitat preservation and responsible breeding programs to reduce the pressure on wild populations.

Understanding the natural habitat and behavior of leopard tortoises is key to appreciating their role in the ecosystem and ensuring their welfare in captivity. By mimicking their native conditions and respecting their natural instincts, owners can provide a healthy and enriching environment for these remarkable reptiles.

Behavior and Social Structure of Leopard Tortoises in the Wild

Leopard tortoises (*Stigmochelys pardalis*) exhibit fascinating behavioral traits and social structures that are crucial to their survival in the wild. Although they are solitary creatures by nature, their behaviors are intricately linked to their environment and social interactions, particularly during breeding season. Understanding these behaviors can help in replicating their needs in captivity to ensure they thrive in a domestic setting.

Behavior in the Wild

1. Feeding and Grazing Habits
Leopard tortoises are herbivores, primarily grazing on grasses, leaves, flowers, and some succulents. Their strong jaws are adapted to tear tough vegetation, which is an essential part of their diet.

- **Foraging Patterns**: They are opportunistic feeders, meaning they will eat whatever vegetation is available, depending on the season. In their natural habitats, where food availability fluctuates with the rains, they may have to travel long distances to find adequate food sources.
- **Feeding Time**: Leopard tortoises are diurnal, meaning they are active during the day. Early mornings and late afternoons are their most active times for foraging, as the heat of midday can be overwhelming. They may graze for several hours, pausing to bask in the sun to regulate their body temperature.
- **Water Acquisition**: While they do not drink water every day, leopard tortoises are excellent at conserving moisture. They

obtain water mainly from the vegetation they consume, as well as from morning dew and seasonal rains. This ability to go long periods without drinking makes them particularly suited to arid environments.

2. Basking and Thermoregulation

Leopard tortoises, like all reptiles, are ectothermic, meaning they rely on external heat sources to regulate their body temperature. In the wild, they spend a significant amount of time basking in the sun to maintain the appropriate body temperature for metabolic processes.

- **Basking Behavior**: Leopard tortoises are known for seeking out sunny spots during the cooler morning and late afternoon hours, usually in open areas such as savannas or grasslands. Basking helps them absorb heat, which is vital for digestion, mobility, and overall health.
- **Shelter Seeking**: When the temperatures rise too high during midday, leopard tortoises seek shelter under bushes, rocks, or trees, where they can escape the direct sun and avoid overheating.

3. Mating and Reproductive Behavior

The mating season for leopard tortoises typically coincides with the rainy season, which provides ample food and moisture for the tortoises to be more active.

Courtship: Males often exhibit a variety of courtship behaviors to attract females. This may include vocalizations, where males produce loud "rattling" sounds, as well as displaying a series of movements that demonstrate their strength and readiness for mating. Males may also engage in head-bobbing or attempt to nudge the female's shell during mating rituals.

Territoriality and Mating Competitions: Male leopard tortoises can be territorial, particularly during the breeding season. They may compete for access to females, with males engaging in head-to-head battles or "ramming" behaviors. These interactions are not typically violent but involve a display of strength.

Nesting and Egg Laying: After mating, females lay their eggs in burrows that they dig in sandy or loose soil. The eggs are buried for protection, and after an incubation period (which can last several months), hatchlings emerge and are vulnerable to a variety of predators.

4. Movement and Range

Leopard tortoises are known for their relatively slow but

deliberate movements, primarily focused on finding food and seeking shelter.

Home Range: While they are not territorial in the sense of defending a specific area, leopard tortoises do have home ranges where they live and forage. These ranges can vary in size depending on the availability of food and water. The size of their range also depends on environmental factors like climate and seasonal changes.

Migration: Leopard tortoises do not undertake long migrations, but they may move across their range seasonally to find more food during periods of drought or after the rains have stopped. They may travel several miles in search of food, water, and suitable nesting sites.

5. Social Structure and Interactions

Leopard tortoises are generally solitary animals, and social interactions between individuals are limited outside of mating season. They do not form permanent social groups or herds like some other species of tortoises or animals. However, there are specific times of the year and specific behaviors that show how they interact with each other.

Solitary Nature: Outside of the breeding season, leopard tortoises tend to be solitary creatures. They do not rely on social structures for survival. Most of their time is spent foraging, basking, and seeking shelter independently.

Social Behavior During Breeding: During the mating season, males will actively seek out females. While males may display competitive behaviors, once mating has occurred, the tortoises return to their solitary lifestyles.

Non-Aggressive Interactions: Though they may display some territorial behaviors during the mating season, leopard tortoises are not particularly aggressive and do not fight over territory. They are usually content to share space as long as there are no threats or competition for resources.

Predators and Survival Tactics

Despite their large size and tough shells, leopard tortoises face a variety of natural predators in the wild, including large carnivores, birds of prey, and humans. To survive, they employ several strategies:

Camouflage: Their spotted shell pattern helps them blend in with the environment, making it harder for predators to spot them in the wild grasses and scrublands.

Speed and Hiding: When threatened, leopard tortoises can retract into their shells for protection. While they are not particularly fast movers, they can quickly retreat into the safety of a burrow or dense vegetation if needed.

Longevity: Tortoises have long lifespans, which increases their chances of surviving into adulthood when they are less vulnerable to predation.

Leopard tortoises are solitary yet resilient creatures with distinct behavioral patterns that allow them to thrive in a variety of African habitats. Their natural instincts—such as their grazing habits, basking behavior, and reproduction strategies—are essential for their survival. While they are not social animals in the traditional sense, the seasonal interactions during breeding periods highlight the complex, yet fascinating, nature of their social structures. Understanding these behaviors is key to caring for leopard tortoises in captivity, ensuring that their environment mimics the conditions of the wild as closely as possible.

Chapter Two

Leopard Tortoise Anatomy and Characteristics

Leopard tortoises (Stigmochelys pardalis) are one of the most distinctive and fascinating species of tortoises, primarily due to their striking physical appearance and unique biological features. Understanding their anatomy is crucial for providing proper care and appreciating the specialized adaptations that allow them to survive in their natural habitats.

Physical Features of Leopard Tortoises

1. Shell (Carapace)

The most notable feature of the leopard tortoise is its high-domed shell, which provides both protection and a unique visual characteristic.

- Shape and Structure: The carapace (top shell) is dome-shaped, which is typical of tortoises, offering protection from predators. It is thick and rigid, made from keratin, the same protein found in human nails. The shape of the shell is designed to help the tortoise navigate the open terrain where they live, providing structural support for their body and protection from harsh environmental elements.

- Shell Pattern: The shell is characterized by its stunning pattern of yellow and black or dark brown spots and streaks, resembling the spots on a leopard's fur. This gives the tortoise its name and helps it blend into the surrounding grasslands and scrublands, offering a form of camouflage against predators. The shell's pattern can vary slightly between individuals, but all leopard tortoises share this striking, mottled appearance.

- Growth and Size: As the tortoise ages, its shell grows with it. It is important to note that the shell is not a separate structure; it is part of the tortoise's skeleton and is attached to its spine and ribcage. The growth rings visible on the shell can indicate the age of the tortoise, similar to tree rings, although these are not always definitive in older tortoises.

- Scutes: The shell is made up of individual plates called scutes. These scutes are hard and protect the tortoise from injury. Each scute is surrounded by a thin, keratinized layer that continues to grow as the tortoise matures.

2. Head and Beak

The leopard tortoise's head is relatively small in proportion to its large body, but it still plays an important role in its feeding and overall survival.

- Shape: The head is oval-shaped with a slightly pointed snout. Unlike some other tortoises, the leopard tortoise does not have a hinged jaw that allows it to retract its head completely into its shell.
- Beak: Instead of teeth, leopard tortoises possess a sharp, beak-like mouth, which is used for cutting and tearing through vegetation. This beak is well-adapted for their herbivorous diet, allowing them to feed on grasses, leaves, and succulents. The sharp edges of the beak help them slice through tough plant matter.
- Eyes and Vision: The leopard tortoise has relatively large eyes, which provide them with good vision, especially for spotting potential threats. They are also able to detect movement and notice changes in their surroundings, although their vision is generally more focused on objects within their close vicinity.
- Nostrils: The tortoise's nostrils are located near the front of the head, allowing them to breathe while foraging or eating. Their sense of smell helps them detect food sources, but their vision is their primary means of navigating the environment.

3. Limbs and Feet

Leopard tortoises have strong, muscular limbs, specially adapted to their terrestrial lifestyle and environment.

- Front Legs (Forelimbs): The front limbs of the leopard tortoise are stout and heavily muscled, designed for digging and supporting their large bodies. The forelegs are equipped with sharp, curved claws, which are used for digging shallow burrows for shelter, laying eggs, and foraging. These claws also help in pushing through dense vegetation.
- Rear Legs (Hindlimbs): The hind limbs are strong and are shaped to allow the tortoise to pull itself forward effectively. These legs also help provide balance when walking and are also equipped with strong claws to support the tortoise's weight.
- Feet: Leopard tortoises have flat, wide feet that help them navigate the ground and distribute their weight evenly. Their feet are also adapted to walking on rugged, uneven terrain. Unlike aquatic turtles, the feet are not webbed but rather designed for land-based movement.

4. Tail

The tail of a leopard tortoise is relatively short and stubby, typically measuring only a few inches in length. The tail serves several functions:

- Reproductive Function: In males, the tail is slightly longer and more pronounced, as it is used during mating. The tail houses the cloacal opening, through which both excretory and reproductive processes occur.
- Protection: While the tail itself does not provide significant protection, it is tucked under the shell when the tortoise retracts its limbs and head, helping to shield it from predators.

5. Internal Anatomy

Leopard tortoises, like all reptiles, have a highly specialized internal anatomy suited to their diet and environment.

- Respiratory System: Being reptiles, leopard tortoises have lungs and rely on air for respiration. However, they are adapted to conserve oxygen and can hold their breath for extended periods, especially when hiding or underwater.
- Digestive System: Their digestive system is designed to break down fibrous plant material. They have a relatively slow metabolism, which allows them to process large amounts of plant matter. Their intestines extract the necessary nutrients from their herbivorous diet, which consists primarily of grasses, herbs, and some fruits or flowers.
- Skeletal System: The leopard tortoise's skeleton is reinforced with a robust ribcage and spine, providing support for its heavy

shell. The shell itself is attached to the spine and ribs, offering structural protection. Unlike some reptiles, tortoises are not capable of shedding or regenerating parts of their shell.

6. Sensory Abilities

Though leopard tortoises are not known for having highly developed sensory systems compared to some other animals, they do possess the senses necessary for survival:

- Vision: Their relatively large eyes help them detect movement and navigate through their environment. While they may not have sharp, far-reaching vision, they are adept at recognizing objects within their immediate surroundings, such as food or potential predators.
- Smell: Their sense of smell is strong and helps them locate food and detect the presence of predators.
- Hearing: Tortoises do not have external ears, but they do have an internal ear structure that allows them to sense vibrations and low-frequency sounds in their environment.

7. Lifespan and Growth

Leopard tortoises are long-lived, with lifespans ranging between 50 to 80 years in the wild, and sometimes even longer in captivity. Their growth is gradual and occurs over many years, with significant growth during the first 10–15 years of life. Their shells grow with them, and the overall size of the tortoise increases steadily as it matures.

The leopard tortoise's anatomy is perfectly designed for its terrestrial, herbivorous lifestyle in the African savannas and scrublands. From its protective shell and beak-like mouth to its strong limbs and specialized digestive system, every feature is tailored to help it survive in a variety of environments. Appreciating these anatomical features is crucial for anyone considering keeping a leopard tortoise as a pet, as their care needs must take into account their unique biological requirements.

Lifespan and Growth Patterns of the Leopard Tortoise

The leopard tortoise (*Stigmochelys pardalis*) is known for its impressive lifespan and slow, steady growth patterns, characteristics that distinguish it from many other tortoise species. Understanding the factors influencing their growth and lifespan is crucial for proper care, especially for those who keep them as pets or are involved in conservation efforts. Leopard tortoises have evolved to live long lives, with growth patterns influenced by their diet, environmental conditions, and genetic factors.

Lifespan of the Leopard Tortoise

1. Average Lifespan

Leopard tortoises are known for their long lifespan, typically living between **50 to 80 years** in the wild. In some cases, they can live even longer in captivity when provided with proper care. This long lifespan is characteristic of many tortoise species, as they have slow metabolisms, and their natural defenses (such as their hard, protective shell) help protect them from predators.

> **Wild vs. Captivity Lifespan**: In the wild, the lifespan of leopard tortoises may be slightly shorter due to natural threats such as predators, disease, and environmental stressors. In captivity, however, with proper care—such as a controlled environment, regular feeding, and protection from predators—these tortoises can live to be well over 80 years old, with some even reaching 100 years or more.

2. Factors Influencing Lifespan

Several factors influence the lifespan of leopard tortoises, including:

Genetics: Like all species, the genetics of individual tortoises plays a role in how long they will live. Healthy tortoises with strong genetic backgrounds are likely to live longer.

Diet and Nutrition: A balanced, nutrient-rich diet is vital for their long-term health. In the wild, they feed on grasses, succulents, and leaves, and in captivity, they need a similar diet supplemented with calcium for healthy shell development.

Environmental Conditions: Tortoises that live in areas with consistent temperature and humidity levels (whether in the wild or captivity) tend to have longer, healthier lives. Inappropriate environmental conditions, such as poor lighting, low temperatures, or insufficient space, can significantly reduce their lifespan.

Predation and Disease: In the wild, predators such as large carnivores, birds of prey, and even humans (through illegal poaching) can impact their survival. Disease and parasitic infections can also shorten their lifespan, particularly in younger tortoises or those in captivity with compromised immune systems.

Growth Patterns of the Leopard Tortoise

Leopard tortoises experience slow and steady growth over the course of their lives. This gradual growth pattern is typical of many long-lived reptiles. Understanding the phases of growth and how they develop can help owners ensure their pets are growing healthily.

1. Early Life and Hatchling Growth

The early stages of a leopard tortoise's life are crucial to its growth and overall health. Hatchlings are typically about **2 to 3 inches (5 to 7 cm)** long at birth, and they are incredibly vulnerable to predation. They are highly dependent on their environment for food and hydration, and the first few years of their lives are critical for survival.

- **Hatchling Growth Rate**: In the first few years, leopard tortoises grow relatively quickly compared to their later years. During this period, they add about **1 to 2 inches (2.5 to 5 cm)** of length per year, as long as they are provided with adequate nutrition and proper care.
- **Dietary Needs**: A high-fiber, calcium-rich diet is essential at this stage, as their shells are still developing. Without sufficient calcium, young tortoises can suffer from shell deformities or even metabolic bone disease, a common issue for pet tortoises that are not fed the proper diet.
- **Survival Rates**: While they are small and vulnerable, hatchlings that survive their first few years can grow

rapidly. The early growth phase sets the stage for the rest of their life.

2. Juvenile and Adolescent Growth

From about **3 to 15 years** of age, leopard tortoises continue to grow steadily, but their rate of growth slows significantly compared to their early years. They may still grow by around **1 to 3 inches (2.5 to 7.5 cm)** per year during this stage.

- **Slowing Growth**: As the tortoise matures, its growth rate decreases. This is a natural process as the tortoise approaches its adult size. At around 10 to 15 years of age, a leopard tortoise will have reached about half of its full adult size.
- **Shell Development**: The shell of a juvenile leopard tortoise continues to harden and form distinct growth rings. These rings, similar to tree rings, help indicate the age of the tortoise. By the time the tortoise is in its teenage years, its shell will be much stronger and larger, though still not fully developed.

3. Adult Size and Growth Ceases

By the time leopard tortoises reach **15 to 20 years old**, they are nearing their full adult size. At this point, their growth begins to significantly slow, and by the time they are **25 to 30 years old**, their growth essentially stops. Adult leopard tortoises can reach a length of about **18 to 24 inches (45 to 60 cm)** and weigh between **30 to 50 pounds (14 to 23 kg)**, although some individuals may grow larger.

Full Size: Most leopard tortoises will have reached their full length by the age of 20, though they may continue to fill out and gain weight for several more years.

Shell Hardening: By adulthood, their shell is fully formed and much harder than in their younger years. It offers maximum protection from predators and environmental threats.

Reproductive Maturity: Leopard tortoises become sexually mature at around **15 to 20 years** of age, although some individuals may take longer to reach full maturity. Males often begin displaying mating behaviors, such as head-bobbing or vocalizations, once they are physically mature.

4. Slow Metabolism and Longevity

Leopard tortoises, like other reptiles, have a slow metabolism, which contributes to their long life. Their metabolism decreases as they age, meaning they require less food and energy as they mature. This slow metabolism also affects their growth rate, contributing to the gradual development they experience throughout their lifetime. The fact that they live for so long with such gradual growth allows them to adapt and survive through various environmental changes, which is a trait that many tortoise species share.

Growth Monitoring and Care in Captivity

For pet owners, monitoring the growth of a leopard tortoise is vital to ensure they are developing properly and remaining healthy throughout their lives. Regular check-ups with a veterinarian who specializes in reptiles can help address any concerns related to growth, shell development, and overall health.

1. Diet and Nutrition for Healthy Growth

To promote healthy growth, especially in younger tortoises, a balanced diet is crucial. This should include:

High-fiber grasses and hay for proper digestion.

Calcium-rich foods like leafy greens (e.g., dandelion greens, collard greens) to ensure strong shell development.

Fresh water should always be available for hydration, particularly during periods of active growth.

2. Environmental Conditions

Leopard tortoises need a controlled environment with appropriate lighting (UVB for proper calcium absorption), temperature (75-95°F or 24-35°C), and humidity to ensure proper growth. Providing an appropriate habitat that mimics their natural environment will also contribute to their well-being and growth patterns.

Leopard tortoises are long-lived animals with slow and steady growth patterns, making them fascinating creatures to study and care for. Their growth journey begins rapidly in their early years and slows down as they approach adulthood, with full maturity typically reached by 20 to 30 years. With proper diet, environmental care, and monitoring, leopard tortoises can live long, healthy lives, making them a rewarding pet for those who are committed to their care.

Chapter Three

Diet and Nutrition for Leopard Tortoises

Leopard tortoises (*Stigmochelys pardalis*) are primarily herbivorous grazers with specific dietary needs. Their nutrition plays a critical role in their growth, health, and overall longevity, both in the wild and in captivity. Understanding their dietary requirements, suitable foods, feeding schedules, and the role of supplements is essential for ensuring their well-being.

Suitable Foods for Leopard Tortoises

Leopard tortoises thrive on a high-fiber, low-protein diet that mimics the natural vegetation found in their native habitats, such as savannas and grasslands. Their diet should primarily consist of fibrous plants, with occasional treats to add variety.

1. Staple Foods: Grasses and Hay

Grasses and hay should make up the bulk of a leopard tortoise's diet, as they closely resemble what the tortoise would naturally consume in the wild.

Common Grasses: Timothy grass, Bermuda grass, orchard grass, and fescue grass are excellent choices.

Hay: Dried grasses, such as timothy or Bermuda hay, are great for providing fiber, especially in areas where fresh grasses are not readily available.

Importance: High fiber content aids in proper digestion and prevents shell deformities and metabolic bone disease.

2. Leafy Greens

Fresh leafy greens add variety and essential nutrients to their diet. Suitable options include:

Dandelion greens

Kale (in moderation due to its oxalate content)

Collard greens

Mustard greens

Turnip greens

Endive

Romaine lettuce (avoid iceberg lettuce, as it has little nutritional value)

Tip: Rotate greens to ensure a balanced intake of nutrients and to prevent the tortoise from becoming too reliant on one type.

3. Edible Weeds and Flowers

Weeds and flowers mimic the natural grazing of a leopard tortoise and provide additional nutrients. Suitable choices include:

Clover

Chicory

Plantain weeds

Hibiscus flowers and leaves

Nasturtium

Rose petals (free from pesticides)

Note: Avoid plants sprayed with chemicals, as tortoises are sensitive to toxins.

4. Fruits (Occasional Treats)

Fruits should only be offered sparingly due to their high sugar content, which can disrupt the tortoise's digestive system. Suitable fruits include:

Papaya

Mango

Watermelon (in moderation)

Cactus pads (nopales), which also provide hydration

Limit: Fruits should constitute no more than 5-10% of their diet.

Feeding Schedule for Leopard Tortoises

Creating a consistent feeding schedule is essential to maintain a healthy routine for your leopard tortoise. Their feeding habits should align with their natural grazing tendencies, where they consume food throughout the day.

1. Daily Feeding Routine

Frequency: Offer fresh food daily for juvenile and adult tortoises.

Quantity: Provide enough food to allow the tortoise to graze for 1–2 hours, ensuring they have access to a variety of options. Avoid overfeeding, as obesity can lead to health issues such as fatty liver disease.

Time: Feed them in the morning or early afternoon to coincide with their natural activity periods. Tortoises tend to graze more actively during warmer daylight hours.

2. Special Considerations by Age

Hatchlings (0–2 years): Require frequent meals with a focus on calcium-rich foods for healthy shell development. Feed twice daily in smaller portions.

Juveniles (2–10 years): Feed once daily with a mix of grasses, greens, and occasional treats.

Adults (10+ years): Feeding once daily or every other day is sufficient, as adults have slower metabolisms and may not require as much food.

Supplements and Nutritional Considerations

In captivity, leopard tortoises often miss out on the diverse plant variety available in the wild, so supplements are necessary to fill potential nutritional gaps. Ensuring proper supplementation can prevent deficiencies that lead to serious health issues.

1. Calcium Supplements

Calcium is critical for proper shell and bone development, especially in young and growing tortoises.

Sources:

Calcium powder (without phosphorus) should be sprinkled lightly on their food 2–3 times a week.

Cuttlefish bones can be placed in the enclosure, allowing the tortoise to nibble on them as needed.

Risk of Deficiency: Lack of calcium can result in metabolic bone disease, soft shell syndrome, and stunted growth.

2. Vitamin D3

Vitamin D3 is essential for calcium absorption. Tortoises naturally synthesize Vitamin D3 through exposure to UVB light, but in captivity, artificial supplementation may be necessary.

    Options: Use high-quality UVB lighting or supplement their diet with small doses of Vitamin D3 if UVB exposure is insufficient.

Caution: Over-supplementation can lead to Vitamin D toxicity, so use sparingly and as recommended by a reptile veterinarian.

3. Multivitamin Supplements

Occasionally dusting their food with a reptile-safe multivitamin ensures they receive essential vitamins and minerals not present in their regular diet.

    Frequency: Use once a week for juveniles and adults, and twice a week for hatchlings.

Note: Choose a product specifically designed for reptiles to avoid harmful additives.

4. Hydration and Water Requirements

Leopard tortoises require constant access to fresh, clean water for drinking and soaking.

Hydration Sources:

Provide a shallow water dish that is easy for the tortoise to access.

Mist their enclosure or provide a humid hide to prevent dehydration, especially for hatchlings and juveniles.

Many leafy greens and succulents naturally provide moisture.

Soaking: Offer weekly soaks in lukewarm water to help with hydration and aid in shedding dead skin or shell scutes.

Foods to Avoid

Certain foods are harmful to leopard tortoises and should never be included in their diet:

High-protein foods: Dog or cat food, legumes, or any animal-based products can damage their kidneys and lead to shell deformities.

Toxic plants: Avoid avocado, rhubarb, oleander, azaleas, and daffodils.

Processed foods: Bread, pasta, or any human snacks are inappropriate and can upset their digestive system.

Lettuce: Iceberg lettuce should be avoided due to its low nutritional value.

A leopard tortoise's diet must prioritize high-fiber, calcium-rich foods to ensure proper growth, shell strength, and overall health. A consistent feeding schedule and the inclusion of supplements like calcium and Vitamin D3 help fill nutritional gaps, especially in captivity. Avoiding harmful foods and maintaining hydration will keep your tortoise thriving for decades. Proper diet and nutrition are the foundation of a healthy and happy leopard tortoise, ensuring they live long and vibrant lives.

Foods to Avoid for Leopard Tortoises

Leopard tortoises are herbivores with specific dietary requirements, and feeding them the wrong foods can lead to serious health issues. There are certain foods and substances that should be strictly avoided, as they can cause digestive problems, toxicity, or long-term health complications. This section outlines the foods that are harmful or unsuitable for leopard tortoises and provides explanations for why they should be excluded from their diet.

1. High-Protein Foods

Leopard tortoises are not designed to handle high-protein diets, as excessive protein can lead to various health problems. In their natural environment, they feed mostly on grasses, leafy greens, and some weeds, which contain very low levels of protein. Feeding high-protein foods can result in kidney damage, shell deformities, and metabolic imbalances.

Foods to Avoid:

- **Animal-based Proteins**: Tortoises should not eat any form of meat, including insects, worms, or fish. These foods are inappropriate for their digestive system.
- **Processed Meats**: Ham, bacon, chicken, or any processed meats are highly unsuitable.
- **Legumes**: Beans (such as kidney beans, chickpeas, or lentils) and peas contain high levels of protein and can be harmful if consumed regularly.
- **Eggs**: While not inherently dangerous in small quantities, eggs are too rich in protein and should be avoided.

Why to Avoid:

 High-protein diets can lead to **kidney damage** over time, as the tortoise's kidneys must work harder to process excess protein. This can also cause **shell deformities** and **metabolic disorders** due to an imbalance in calcium and phosphorus levels. Additionally, excess protein leads to fat accumulation, contributing to obesity.

2. Toxic Plants

There are many plants that are toxic to leopard tortoises, and consuming them can cause poisoning or even death. While many plants are edible for humans or other animals, they can be harmful to tortoises.

Common Toxic Plants to Avoid:

- **Avocado**: Contains a substance called **persin**, which is toxic to many animals, including tortoises. It can cause respiratory issues, heart failure, and even death if ingested in significant amounts.
- **Rhubarb**: All parts of the rhubarb plant (especially the leaves) are toxic to tortoises, containing high levels of **oxalates** and **anthraquinone glycosides**, which can cause kidney failure and digestive issues.

Oleander: A common ornamental plant, **oleander** is highly toxic to tortoises and can lead to severe heart and digestive issues.

Azaleas: These plants contain **grayanotoxins**, which can cause vomiting, diarrhea, and even death.

Daffodils: All parts of the daffodil, including the leaves, flowers, and bulbs, are toxic to tortoises, leading to gastrointestinal issues and lethargy.

Foxglove: Contains **digitalis glycosides**, which can be fatal if ingested, affecting the heart and nervous system.

Why to Avoid:

These plants contain **toxins** that can cause immediate or long-term damage to the tortoise's digestive system, kidneys, or cardiovascular system. In severe cases, ingestion of toxic plants can be fatal. It's crucial to be aware of the plants in your environment and ensure that any plants or flowers accessible to your tortoise are safe.

3. Lettuce (Iceberg and Other Varieties)

Lettuce, particularly **iceberg lettuce**, offers very little nutritional value to leopard tortoises. While many tortoises enjoy the taste of lettuce, it can be harmful if used as a major part of their diet.

Types of Lettuce to Avoid:

Iceberg lettuce: Contains a very low level of vitamins and nutrients, and it's mostly water. It can cause diarrhea and dehydration.

Other lettuce varieties (in excess): Romaine and butterhead lettuce are better than iceberg but still offer limited nutritional value and should only be fed in moderation.

Why to Avoid:

Low Nutritional Value: Iceberg lettuce and similar varieties lack the essential vitamins and minerals tortoises need for healthy growth. They are predominantly water, which can fill the tortoise's stomach without providing sufficient calories or nutrients.

Potential for Diarrhea: Lettuce's high water content can cause gastrointestinal issues, such as diarrhea, particularly in juvenile tortoises, which are more sensitive to dietary changes.

4. Fruit (In Excess)

While fruit can be an occasional treat for leopard tortoises, it should be given sparingly. Many fruits contain high levels of **sugar**, which can disrupt the tortoise's digestive system and lead to obesity.

Fruits to Limit or Avoid:

Apples: While not inherently harmful, apples are sugary, and
consuming them too often can contribute to obesity and
upset the tortoise's digestive system.

Pineapple: Pineapple is high in sugar and acidity, which can
cause digestive issues in tortoises.

Bananas: High in sugar and potassium, bananas should only be
offered as an occasional treat.

Grapes: Grapes are also high in sugar and should be avoided
in large amounts.

Why to Avoid in Excess:

High Sugar Content: Excess sugar can lead to **obesity, fatty
liver disease**, and metabolic problems, which are common
in tortoises fed a fruit-heavy diet.

Digestive Problems: A high intake of sugary fruits can cause
diarrhea and **stomach upset**, especially in younger
tortoises.

5. Processed and Human Foods

Feeding leopard tortoises processed or human foods can cause a
host of problems, ranging from digestive upset to long-term health
issues. These foods lack the essential nutrients tortoises require and

often contain additives, preservatives, and seasonings that are toxic to reptiles.

Processed Foods to Avoid:

Bread: Bread contains gluten and carbohydrates, which can cause bloating and digestive problems. It offers no real nutritional benefit for a tortoise and can contribute to obesity.

Pasta: Like bread, pasta is high in carbohydrates and lacks the nutrients tortoises need.

Cereals: Breakfast cereals often contain sugars and preservatives that are harmful to tortoises.

Potatoes: Raw potatoes contain **solanine**, a toxic substance that can cause lethargy, digestive issues, and even death.

Salty Foods: Processed foods like chips, pretzels, or anything high in salt should be avoided as excessive salt can be toxic.

Why to Avoid:

Lack of Nutritional Value: Processed foods lack the essential vitamins and minerals needed for a healthy tortoise.

Harmful Additives: Ingredients like salt, preservatives, and artificial flavorings can be toxic to tortoises and lead to dehydration, kidney problems, and long-term damage.

Obesity and Digestive Issues: High-carbohydrate and high-sugar foods can contribute to obesity and digestive problems, especially when fed regularly.

6. Spinach and Other Oxalate-Rich Greens

While spinach is not toxic to tortoises, it contains **oxalates**, which can interfere with calcium absorption and contribute to kidney problems if fed in large quantities.

Greens to Avoid or Limit:

Spinach

Swiss chard

Beet greens

Rhubarb leaves (as mentioned above, rhubarb is also toxic in large amounts)

Why to Avoid:

Oxalates: These compounds bind to calcium and prevent its absorption, potentially leading to **calcium deficiency** and causing issues like **metabolic bone disease**.

Kidney Damage: Excessive oxalates can also lead to **kidney stones** and kidney damage over time.

To ensure your leopard tortoise stays healthy, it's essential to avoid foods that could harm them. A diet focused on high-fiber grasses, leafy greens, and edible plants is the best way to meet their nutritional needs. By avoiding high-protein foods, toxic plants, fruits in excess, and processed human foods, you can help prevent obesity, kidney damage, digestive issues, and other health problems. Careful attention to diet is a critical part of providing the long, healthy life that leopard tortoises are known for.

Chapter Four

Setting Up the Ideal Habitat for a Leopard Tortoise: Indoor vs Outdoor Enclosures

Creating an appropriate and comfortable habitat for your leopard tortoise is crucial for its well-being. Leopard tortoises are native to the dry, semi-arid savannas of East Africa, where they roam in hot, sunny environments with access to areas of shade. Replicating this environment as closely as possible, whether indoors or outdoors, will help your tortoise thrive. Below, we'll explore the key factors to consider when setting up either an indoor or outdoor enclosure, comparing the two options.

1. Indoor Enclosures for Leopard Tortoises

Indoor enclosures provide a controlled environment, especially for owners who live in climates unsuitable for outdoor enclosures year-round. However, creating an ideal indoor setup requires careful attention to lighting, temperature, humidity, and space.

Key Considerations for Indoor Enclosures:

a. Size and Space

- Leopard tortoises need **ample space** to roam and graze. A general rule of thumb is that the enclosure should be at least **4–6 times the length of the tortoise** in width, and **2–3 times its length** in length. For example, a full-grown leopard tortoise that measures 12 inches in length should have an enclosure that is at least **4 feet by 6 feet** in size.
- **Larger enclosures** provide the tortoise with more opportunities for exercise and grazing, which is critical for maintaining a healthy weight and promoting good shell development.
- For juveniles, a smaller space can be used but should be upgraded as the tortoise grows.

b. Temperature and Lighting

Leopard tortoises are cold-blooded reptiles, which means they rely on external sources of heat to regulate their body temperature. Proper **temperature gradients** are vital.

> **Basking area**: Set up a basking area where the temperature is between **90-95°F (32-35°C)**. This allows the tortoise to regulate its body temperature.

> **Cool side**: The cooler end of the enclosure should be around **75–80°F (24–27°C)**.

> **Night temperature**: During the night, temperatures can drop to **70°F (21°C)**.

Provide **UVB lighting** to ensure your tortoise can synthesize vitamin D3, which is essential for calcium absorption and shell health. Use a **UVB bulb** that provides both UVA and UVB rays, and position it over the basking area to simulate natural sunlight.

If you do not have access to natural sunlight, **UVB lamps** should be replaced every **6–12 months** to maintain their effectiveness.

c. Substrate

The choice of **substrate** is essential for creating a natural and healthy environment. Suitable substrates for indoor enclosures include:

Coconut coir: Absorbent, easy to clean, and provides a natural feel.

Cypress mulch: A natural substrate that holds moisture, helping to maintain humidity.

Organic topsoil mixed with sand: Provides a more natural feel and encourages digging, which is typical behavior for leopard tortoises.

Avoid: Using substrates like **cedar wood chips** or **sand** alone, as they can be harmful to tortoises and can cause respiratory or digestive issues.

d. Humidity and Hydration

Leopard tortoises come from dry climates, so they do not need a high-humidity environment. However, it is essential to maintain a level of **moderate humidity** (around **40-60%**), especially for younger tortoises or if you are using a soil-based substrate.

Provide a shallow water dish for drinking and soaking. The dish should be shallow enough to prevent drowning, but large enough to allow the tortoise to soak its body.

Regular misting can help maintain humidity, especially if the enclosure is dry due to heating systems.

e. Enclosure Furniture and Enrichment

Offer hiding spots, such as **clay pots** or **wooden hides**, to help your tortoise feel secure. Tortoises appreciate areas to retreat to, especially during the night.

Include rocks, logs, or safe plants for climbing and grazing. A **gentle slope** in the habitat allows your tortoise to climb and exercise, promoting strong legs and shell growth.

2. Outdoor Enclosures for Leopard Tortoises

Outdoor enclosures provide a more natural environment for your leopard tortoise, offering access to sunlight, natural vegetation, and larger space for movement. However, outdoor enclosures require careful planning to ensure they are secure and provide proper shelter from extreme weather conditions.

Key Considerations for Outdoor Enclosures:

a. Size and Space

Outdoor enclosures can be significantly larger than indoor setups, and size is one of the biggest advantages. A **minimum of 8 feet by 8 feet** is recommended for a single adult leopard tortoise. If possible, larger enclosures (20 feet by 20 feet or more) allow for more natural roaming space, which benefits the tortoise's health and well-being.

Fencing is critical for an outdoor enclosure to prevent the tortoise from escaping or being preyed upon by other animals. The fence should be at least **18–24 inches tall**, and the bottom should be buried to prevent the tortoise from digging underneath.

b. Temperature and Weather Conditions

Climate considerations: Leopard tortoises are adapted to hot, dry environments. If you live in a **warm climate**, an outdoor enclosure can provide the heat and sunlight they need to thrive. However, in areas with **cold winters**, outdoor enclosures might not be feasible without special measures to protect the tortoise during the colder months.

If outdoor temperatures regularly dip below **50°F (10°C)**, it's essential to provide an **indoor shelter** for the tortoise during the winter.

Shading: Provide access to shaded areas to allow the tortoise to regulate its body temperature during hot weather.

c. Natural Elements and Vegetation

Outdoor enclosures can include **natural plants**, grasses, and weeds, which your tortoise can graze on, just like it would in the wild. Some safe plants include dandelions, clover, and plantains, which can provide natural nutrition.

Avoid toxic plants such as avocado, rhubarb, and azaleas, as mentioned earlier, and make sure the enclosure is free of any potential hazards.

Include natural features like **rocks**, **logs**, and **dirt mounds** to provide enrichment, promote exercise, and mimic the tortoise's natural environment.

d. Shelter and Protection

Even in an outdoor enclosure, your tortoise will need access to shelter to protect it from extreme weather conditions. A **sheltered area** with a waterproof roof or covered hide will keep your tortoise safe from rain, extreme heat, and cold. It should be large enough for the tortoise to retreat to if it needs to cool down or warm up.

Ensure the shelter provides proper **ventilation** and has a **soft substrate**, such as hay or leaves, to make it comfortable for the tortoise.

e. Security and Safety

Outdoor enclosures need to be **secure** to prevent predators from entering, such as dogs, birds of prey, or raccoons.

Fencing must be sturdy and buried into the ground to prevent tunneling.

Predator-proofing: Consider using hardware cloth or strong wire mesh with small openings to keep out animals while allowing air circulation.

Additionally, the enclosure should be **escape-proof** since tortoises are adept at finding ways out, especially if they feel threatened.

Both indoor and outdoor enclosures have their advantages and challenges, and the ideal choice depends largely on your climate, available space, and the specific needs of your leopard tortoise. Indoor enclosures are perfect for providing a controlled environment year-round, especially in cooler climates, while outdoor enclosures provide a more natural habitat with ample space and sunlight. The key is to provide a **safe, comfortable, and enriching environment** that closely mimics the tortoise's natural habitat to ensure it remains healthy and active.

Temperature, Humidity, Lighting, and UVB Needs for Leopard Tortoises

Leopard tortoises, native to the dry, hot savannas and semi-arid regions of East Africa, have specific environmental needs when it comes to **temperature**, **humidity**, **lighting**, and **UVB** exposure. These factors are crucial for maintaining their overall health, promoting proper digestion, shell growth, and metabolic function. Below, we will explore each of these requirements in detail.

1. Temperature Requirements for Leopard Tortoises

Temperature is one of the most important aspects of a leopard tortoise's care. As ectothermic (cold-blooded) reptiles, they rely on external sources of heat to regulate their body temperature, which directly affects their metabolic rate, digestion, and activity levels. Leopard tortoises require a **temperature gradient** in their habitat, allowing them to move between warmer and cooler areas as needed to maintain optimal health.

Ideal Temperature Range:

Basking Area:

The basking area is where the tortoise will go to raise its body temperature. This area should be maintained between **90°F to 95°F (32°C to 35°C)**. Basking helps the tortoise digest food properly, synthesize vitamins, and maintain metabolic functions. It is important that the basking spot is **directly under a heat source** (such as a basking lamp) to provide this heat.

Cooler Area:

A cooler area in the enclosure, away from the basking spot, should be maintained at **75°F to 80°F (24°C to 27°C)**. This area provides a temperature range where the tortoise can retreat when it feels too hot or needs to regulate its body temperature. This cooler area is also essential for their overall comfort and to avoid overheating.

Nighttime Temperature:

Leopard tortoises are adapted to cooler temperatures at night, so nighttime temperatures can drop to **70°F (21°C)**, with no lower than **65°F (18°C)**. It's important not to allow the enclosure to cool too much overnight, as it could stress the tortoise and impact its immune system. If nighttime temperatures in your home or outdoor area fall lower than this range, supplemental heating should be provided.

How to Achieve Proper Temperature:

Basking Lamp: Use a **heat lamp** (such as a halogen or incandescent bulb) to create a basking spot that achieves the necessary heat. These bulbs should be positioned above the basking area and replaced regularly to maintain consistent heat output.

Heat Mats and Ceramic Heat Emitters: These can also help maintain the correct ambient temperature in cooler climates or indoor setups.

Thermometers: Use thermometers placed at both the basking and cooler areas to ensure the temperature gradient is appropriate.

Night Heating: In colder climates or during the winter, use a **ceramic heat emitter** or **reptile heat pad** to maintain temperatures overnight, without producing light that could disturb the tortoise's sleep cycle.

2. Humidity Requirements for Leopard Tortoises

Leopard tortoises are native to semi-arid regions, meaning they are adapted to relatively **low humidity** levels. However, they do require **moderate humidity** to support their overall health, particularly to prevent issues like dehydration or shedding problems.

Ideal Humidity Range:

The ideal humidity level for leopard tortoises should be **40-60%**. This is especially important for younger tortoises, as they are more sensitive to changes in humidity and need adequate moisture levels to help with shedding and respiratory health.

Humidity too high: Excessive humidity (above 70%) can cause respiratory problems, fungal infections, and shell rot. It can also encourage mold growth in the substrate, which can be dangerous to your tortoise.

Humidity too low: On the other hand, extremely low humidity (below 30%) can lead to dehydration, particularly in younger tortoises, and cause shedding problems, such as incomplete or stuck shed skin. Dehydration can also impact digestion, making it harder for the tortoise to process its food.

How to Maintain Ideal Humidity:

Regular Misting: Mist the enclosure once or twice a day using a **fine spray bottle** to add moisture to the air. Be sure not to over-wet the enclosure; the goal is to maintain consistent but moderate humidity.

Water Dish: Always provide a **shallow water dish** in the enclosure. This allows the tortoise to drink and also soak if desired, helping to maintain hydration. Ensure the water is shallow enough that the tortoise can't drown.

Humidity Monitors: Use a **hygrometer** to monitor the humidity level in the enclosure. This will help ensure that the humidity stays within the ideal range and prevent any health problems.

3. Lighting and UVB Needs for Leopard Tortoises

Like all reptiles, leopard tortoises require proper lighting to regulate their biological functions, including digestion, sleep cycles, and the synthesis of **vitamin D3**. Exposure to ultraviolet B (UVB) light is especially important for reptiles because it allows them to synthesize vitamin D3, which is crucial for calcium absorption and bone health.

Importance of UVB Light:

Vitamin D3 Production: UVB light allows tortoises to produce vitamin D3 in their skin, which is necessary for absorbing calcium from their diet. Without adequate UVB exposure, a tortoise may develop **metabolic bone disease**, a condition that causes weak bones, soft shells, and other serious health issues.

Regulation of Biological Processes: UVB light also helps regulate the tortoise's sleep-wake cycle (circadian rhythm) and supports other metabolic processes.

Ideal UVB Lighting for Leopard Tortoises:

Leopard tortoises require **direct UVB exposure** for about **10-12 hours per day** to ensure they are getting enough of this vital light.

UVB Bulbs: Use a high-quality **UVB bulb** specifically designed for reptiles. The most effective types are **tube-style UVB bulbs** or **compact fluorescent bulbs** that emit UVB radiation. These should be placed **no further than 12-18 inches from the tortoise**.

UVB Lamp Placement: The UVB light should be positioned over the basking area, as this is where the tortoise will naturally seek out warmth and UVB exposure. Ensure that the UVB bulb covers the full length of the basking area for adequate exposure.

How to Choose the Right UVB Bulb:

UVB Output: Select a **UVB 10.0 or 12.0** bulb for best results. These are particularly effective for desert-dwelling reptiles like the leopard tortoise, as they mimic the natural sunlight they would be exposed to in the wild.

Replacement Schedule: UVB bulbs lose their effectiveness over time, even if the light still works. To ensure your tortoise gets adequate UVB exposure, replace the bulb every **6-12 months**, depending on the manufacturer's recommendations. Even though the bulb may still produce visible light, it will no longer emit sufficient UVB after a certain period.

Additional Lighting Considerations:

Day-Night Cycle: Tortoises require a **regular day-night cycle** to simulate natural conditions. Set the UVB and basking lights on a timer so they automatically turn on for **10-12 hours** during the day and off at night to mimic natural light patterns.

Heat Lamps: In addition to UVB lighting, your tortoise will need **heat lamps** to create a basking spot that reaches the appropriate temperature. **Basking bulbs** provide both heat and light, creating an ideal environment for the tortoise to bask in and regulate its body temperature.

Creating the ideal environment for a leopard tortoise involves careful attention to **temperature**, **humidity**, and **UVB lighting**. These elements are essential for maintaining your tortoise's health, promoting healthy bone and shell growth, ensuring proper digestion, and preventing metabolic disorders. By replicating their natural conditions—sunlight, warmth, and moderate humidity— you will provide a habitat that keeps your tortoise active, healthy, and content. Whether housed indoors or outdoors, providing the right lighting, temperature, and humidity will ensure your leopard tortoise lives a long and healthy life.

Chapter Five

Handling and Socializing Your Leopard Tortoise: Proper Handling Techniques

Leopard tortoises are generally gentle and non-aggressive animals. However, handling them properly is essential for their well-being and to ensure that they remain comfortable and stress-free. Unlike some pets, tortoises don't actively seek out interaction, and improper handling can cause them stress, leading to behavioral issues or even health problems. Below, we will cover the best practices for handling your leopard tortoise, how to minimize stress, and when to avoid handling.

1. Understanding Leopard Tortoise Behavior

Before learning the proper techniques for handling your tortoise, it is important to understand their natural behavior and preferences:

Solitary Nature: Leopard tortoises are solitary animals in the wild and typically do not enjoy excessive social interaction. While they may tolerate some handling, it should be done minimally and respectfully.

Slow Movers: Tortoises are slow movers by nature, and they don't usually enjoy being rushed or picked up abruptly. They prefer to move at their own pace and may become anxious if handled too much.

Self-Defense Mechanisms: When a tortoise feels threatened, it may retreat into its shell. This is a natural defense mechanism. Therefore, it's important not to force the tortoise into situations that make it feel cornered or unsafe.

Proper handling techniques focus on making the experience as comfortable and stress-free as possible for the tortoise.

2. When and Why to Handle Your Leopard Tortoise

Handling your leopard tortoise should not be an everyday activity. However, there are times when it is necessary or beneficial:

Routine Health Checks: Periodic health checks are important to ensure your tortoise is healthy. Handling may be needed for basic exams, such as checking its shell, weight, and overall condition.

Cleaning or Moving to a New Enclosure: Sometimes, handling is required when cleaning or moving the tortoise to a new enclosure or a different location.

Training and Socialization: While tortoises are not naturally social creatures, they can get used to human presence and occasional handling with time. Gentle interaction can help build trust and reduce anxiety, making them more comfortable in environments outside their enclosure.

3. Proper Handling Techniques for Leopard Tortoises

a. How to Pick Up Your Leopard Tortoise Safely

The key to handling a leopard tortoise is to be gentle, slow, and always support its body properly. Follow these steps to ensure you're picking it up safely:

Prepare the Tortoise: Approach your tortoise calmly and slowly, allowing it time to sense your presence. Avoid sudden movements or loud noises that may startle it.

Place Your Hands Correctly:

Under the Body: Always **support the tortoise's body** from underneath using both hands. Place one hand under the front of its body, near the **front limbs,**

and the other hand under the back, supporting the **hind limbs**.

Avoid Lifting by the Shell: Never grab or lift a tortoise by its shell, as this can cause internal damage, especially to its spine. The shell is a part of the tortoise's skeleton, and any improper lifting can lead to long-term injury.

Lift Gently and Steadily: Gently lift the tortoise, ensuring that its body is fully supported. Hold it steady and avoid jerky movements that might cause stress or harm. If you need to move the tortoise a longer distance, do so slowly, giving it time to adjust to the new surroundings.

Keep It Close to Your Body: While holding the tortoise, keep it close to your body for stability and warmth. This also reduces the feeling of "exposure," which might cause stress. Hold the tortoise gently and securely, ensuring it feels safe in your hands.

Minimize Height: Try not to hold the tortoise too high above the ground. Doing so can disorient the tortoise, and it might become anxious or fearful of falling. Keeping it close to the ground also reduces the risk of injury if the tortoise were to struggle or be dropped.

b. How to Let the Tortoise Down Safely

When putting the tortoise back in its enclosure, follow these steps:

Set the Tortoise Down Gently: Place the tortoise on the ground slowly and steadily, ensuring its legs and body are fully supported. Avoid dropping the tortoise or letting it fall from a height, as this can cause injury.

Let It Walk Out of Your Hands: Allow the tortoise to walk off your hands rather than placing it abruptly on the ground. This helps it feel more secure and less stressed.

4. Handling Tips to Minimize Stress

a. Keep Handling to a Minimum

Leopard tortoises, like most reptiles, are best left to their own devices most of the time. Overhandling can cause unnecessary stress. Limit handling to no more than **once a week** or when absolutely necessary for health checks or enclosure maintenance. Avoid picking up your tortoise every time you interact with it.

b. Avoid Handling After Eating

Tortoises are sensitive to stress after eating, and handling right after meals can cause them to become anxious or disrupt digestion. It's best to wait at least **30 minutes to 1 hour** after feeding before attempting to handle your tortoise.

c. Be Aware of Temperature

Tortoises are ectothermic and rely on external temperatures to regulate their body heat. If you plan to handle your tortoise, ensure it is not too cold or too hot. Never handle your tortoise in a **cold environment** (below 70°F / 21°C) as this can stress the tortoise and cause health problems like respiratory issues. Similarly, avoid handling during extremely hot weather as it can overheat the tortoise.

d. Watch for Signs of Stress

It's important to be aware of your tortoise's behavior when handling it. If it begins to show signs of stress, such as:

Pulling into its shell

Kicking its legs

Trying to escape

Rapid breathing or vocalizing

Stop handling immediately. Give your tortoise time to calm down, and always ensure that your interactions are calm and gentle.

5. Socializing Your Leopard Tortoise

Leopard tortoises are not naturally social and do not seek out companionship or interaction with humans or other animals. However, they can become accustomed to human presence with consistent, gentle handling.

Building Trust:

- **Allow Time for Adjustment**: If you've just brought your leopard tortoise home, give it time to adjust to its new environment. Limit handling initially to let the tortoise acclimate to its habitat.
- **Slow, Positive Interactions**: Start with short, positive interactions. Gently approach and offer food or let the tortoise explore your hand or arm without picking it up. Over time, it will become more comfortable with your presence.
- **Patience is Key**: Socializing a leopard tortoise takes time. Be patient, and let your tortoise decide when it's ready for more interaction.

Do Leopard Tortoises Get Along with Other Pets?

While leopard tortoises are usually solitary animals, some individuals may tolerate other tortoises or even certain types of animals, such as reptiles. However, they should never be housed with aggressive or highly active pets, such as dogs or cats, as this could lead to stress or injury. Always monitor the behavior of all pets in the household to ensure there is no undue stress caused to your tortoise.

Proper handling and socializing are important aspects of caring for your leopard tortoise. By using the right techniques—such as supporting the tortoise's body, minimizing handling time, and watching for signs of stress—you can ensure your tortoise remains comfortable and healthy. Remember, while leopard tortoises may become accustomed to their human caregivers, they are not naturally social animals, and excessive handling should be avoided. By creating a respectful, safe, and low-stress environment, you'll help your leopard tortoise live a long and happy life.

Socialization and Interaction Tips for Leopard Tortoises

While leopard tortoises are solitary creatures by nature, they can still become accustomed to human presence and certain types of interaction. Socializing and interacting with your tortoise should always be done gently and in a way that respects their natural instincts and behaviors. Here, we will discuss how to approach socialization and interaction with your leopard tortoise, the benefits of doing so, and tips for fostering a positive relationship while ensuring their well-being.

1. Understanding Leopard Tortoise Behavior

Before attempting to interact with or socialize your leopard tortoise, it's important to understand its natural behavior and temperament:

- **Solitary Nature**: Leopard tortoises do not seek social interaction in the way that many mammals do. In the wild, they are solitary animals that are more focused on foraging for food and basking in the sun rather than seeking companionship. As such, they do not require constant attention or companionship from humans.

- **Slow and Cautious Movements**: Leopard tortoises are slow movers and tend to be cautious creatures. They often take their time to explore new environments and stimuli, retreating into their shell when they feel threatened or unsure.

Comfort in Familiarity: While they don't thrive on social interaction, leopard tortoises can get used to human presence and handling over time. Regular, gentle interactions help build trust between you and your tortoise. However, it's important to respect their space and not overwhelm them with excessive handling or interaction.

2. Socializing Your Leopard Tortoise

Socialization is the process of helping your tortoise become comfortable with you, your home, and other environments outside of its enclosure. This process should be gradual and patient. Here's how you can socialize your leopard tortoise:

a. Start Slow: Allow Time for Adjustment

When you first bring your tortoise home, it's crucial to give it time to adjust to its new surroundings. Avoid handling it too much during this initial period. Provide a safe and quiet space where your tortoise can settle in and feel secure in its new environment.

Acclimatization: For the first few days or even weeks, limit interaction and allow the tortoise to get used to its new habitat. Constantly handling it too soon can cause unnecessary stress.

Familiarize with the Environment: Let your tortoise roam around its enclosure and become familiar with the layout and structure. The more comfortable it feels in its space, the more likely it will tolerate future interactions.

b. Gentle, Non-Threatening Interaction

Once your tortoise has acclimated to its new environment, you can begin gentle interactions. These should be calm and slow to avoid startling or scaring your tortoise.

Start with Offering Food: A great way to build trust is by offering food. Place food such as leafy greens or fruits in front of your tortoise, allowing it to associate you with positive experiences (i.e., food).

Let the Tortoise Approach You: Rather than picking up your tortoise immediately, let it come to you. Sit quietly near your tortoise and allow it to explore you at its own pace. Avoid reaching directly for it or moving suddenly, as this could cause stress.

Hand Feeding: Once your tortoise seems comfortable with your presence, you can try hand-feeding it. This further establishes a positive relationship. Hold pieces of food near your tortoise, allowing it to approach your hand at its own pace.

c. Minimal Handling, But Gradual Exposure

While leopard tortoises are not naturally inclined to seek interaction, they can become accustomed to being handled if done correctly.

Handling Sessions: Start with short handling sessions. When you pick up your tortoise (following the proper handling techniques), be sure to keep the interaction calm and brief. Tortoises that are not used to handling can get stressed, so avoid picking them up too frequently, especially in the early stages.

Gentle Movement: During handling, keep movements gentle and slow. Do not shake or move them abruptly. Let your tortoise feel secure in your hands.

Avoid Overhandling: Limit handling to once or twice a week to prevent stress. Overhandling can lead to anxiety and behavioral issues in the tortoise.

3. Building Trust Through Routine

Leopard tortoises are creatures of habit and thrive on routine. A consistent, predictable schedule can help your tortoise feel secure and comfortable in its environment.

Consistent Feeding Times: Feed your tortoise at the same time every day, ideally during daylight hours when it is most active. This routine helps your tortoise associate you with food and positive interactions.

Same Approach Each Time: Approach your tortoise in the same manner each time. Consistent behavior on your part—speaking gently, moving slowly—helps your tortoise recognize you and reduces fear or anxiety.

Quiet, Calm Interactions: Tortoises are more likely to interact with you when you speak in a calm, soothing voice. Avoid loud noises or sudden movements around your tortoise, as this can cause it to retreat into its shell out of fear.

4. Socialization with Other Tortoises

If you have more than one leopard tortoise or plan to introduce others, it's important to proceed carefully, as tortoises can sometimes exhibit territorial behaviors.

- **Separate Introductions**: If introducing a new tortoise to an existing one, do so gradually. Place the tortoises in separate enclosures and allow them to get used to each other's scent before any direct interaction.

- **Observe Behavior**: Leopard tortoises can be territorial and may not always get along with others. Monitor their interactions carefully. Signs of aggression, such as biting, head bobbing, or chasing, should be addressed immediately. If aggression persists, it may be necessary to house them separately.

- **Shared Space**: If you plan on housing multiple tortoises in the same enclosure, ensure there is plenty of space, hiding spots, and access to food to avoid competition and stress. Leopard tortoises, like other tortoises, prefer to have some solitude when eating or resting.

5. Signs of Stress and How to Handle It

Although leopard tortoises are relatively calm animals, they can become stressed if handled incorrectly or excessively. It's essential to recognize the signs of stress in your tortoise and adjust your approach accordingly.

Signs of Stress:

- **Hiding in the Shell**: If your tortoise retreats into its shell and stays there for an extended period, it may be feeling stressed or threatened.
- **Rapid Breathing**: Increased breathing rate, especially if accompanied by other signs of distress, may indicate stress or discomfort.
- **Inactivity**: If your tortoise becomes excessively lethargic or refuses to eat or drink, this could indicate stress or illness.
- **Aggressive Behavior**: Biting, hissing, or attempting to escape can be signs of stress and discomfort.

How to Address Stress:

Reduce Handling: If your tortoise is stressed, give it time to calm down. Reduce handling and interactions until it seems more comfortable.

Provide a Safe Space: Ensure your tortoise has access to hiding spots and shelters within its enclosure to retreat to when it feels threatened or overwhelmed.

Check the Environment: Sometimes stress can be caused by environmental factors, such as temperature or humidity changes. Ensure the habitat conditions are optimal to avoid unnecessary stress.

6. Socializing with Humans and Other Pets

While leopard tortoises are not as social as other animals, they can learn to tolerate human presence and even other pets in the household. However, interactions with other pets, particularly dogs and cats, should always be supervised. Leopard tortoises should never be left alone with potentially predatory animals, as this could lead to stress or injury.

Socializing and interacting with your leopard tortoise requires patience, understanding, and a gentle approach. These animals are not naturally social, but they can learn to tolerate and even enjoy positive, low-stress interactions with their human caregivers. By respecting their natural instincts, providing them with a consistent routine, and monitoring their comfort levels, you can build a trusting relationship with your tortoise. Always prioritize their well-being and minimize handling to ensure they remain healthy, happy, and stress-free.

Chapter Six

Health Care and Common Illnesses: Preventative Care and Vet Visits for Leopard Tortoises

Ensuring the health and well-being of your leopard tortoise requires proactive care, regular check-ups, and attention to environmental factors that may impact its health. While leopard tortoises are generally hardy and resilient, they are still susceptible to certain health issues, especially if their care environment or diet is not properly managed. Preventative care plays a critical role in keeping your tortoise healthy, and regular veterinary visits are an important part of any responsible tortoise owner's routine.

Here's a detailed guide to preventative care for leopard tortoises, including the importance of veterinary visits, common health issues, and how to keep your tortoise in the best shape possible.

1. Understanding Preventative Care for Leopard Tortoises

Preventative care for leopard tortoises focuses on keeping your tortoise healthy through proper husbandry practices and routine care. It is about creating an environment that reduces the risk of illness, monitoring your tortoise's condition regularly, and providing the right nutrients, temperature, and humidity levels.

a. Proper Habitat Management

The foundation of a healthy tortoise is a well-maintained habitat. Leopard tortoises are very sensitive to environmental changes, and improper conditions can lead to stress and illness.

- **Enclosure Size**: Ensure the tortoise's enclosure is spacious enough for it to roam, bask, and exercise. An overcrowded space can lead to behavioral stress and health problems.
- **Temperature and Humidity**: Leopard tortoises require a temperature range of **75°F to 95°F** (24°C to 35°C) during the day, with a cooler nighttime temperature of **65°F to 75°F** (18°C to 24°C). Humidity should be maintained between **50% and 70%**, and a basking spot should reach

95°F to 100°F (35°C to 38°C). Incorrect temperature or humidity levels can lead to respiratory infections or other health complications.

UVB Lighting: Leopard tortoises need access to UVB light for **calcium absorption** and to prevent metabolic bone disease (MBD). Ensure they have access to **UVB lighting** for **10 to 12 hours a day** if kept indoors, and provide natural sunlight if possible when outdoors.

b. Proper Diet and Nutrition

A balanced diet is one of the most crucial aspects of preventative care for your tortoise. A healthy diet helps strengthen your tortoise's immune system, supports proper growth, and prevents nutritional deficiencies.

Leafy Greens: Provide a variety of dark leafy greens like **collard greens**, **dandelion greens**, and **mustard greens**. These should be the foundation of your tortoise's diet.

Vegetables and Fruits: Offer vegetables like **squash**, **cucumber**, and **bell peppers**, and occasionally fruits like **berries**, **apples**, or **melon** as a treat.

Calcium and Vitamin D3: To prevent metabolic bone disease, provide a **calcium supplement** dusted on their food, and ensure they have access to **UVB lighting** to help absorb calcium properly.

Avoid High-Protein Foods: Leopard tortoises are herbivores, and a diet high in protein (e.g., meat, eggs, or high-protein pellets) can lead to kidney damage or other metabolic issues.

c. Regular Cleaning and Hygiene

Keeping the enclosure clean is essential for preventing diseases and parasites. Regularly clean the tortoise's enclosure to remove any waste, uneaten food, and bacteria. A dirty environment can lead to **respiratory infections**, **parasites**, and **skin infections**.

2. Signs of a Healthy Leopard Tortoise

A healthy leopard tortoise should:

Have **clear, bright eyes** with no discharge or swelling.

Display a **shiny, intact shell** without cracks, lesions, or signs of infection.

Be **active and alert**, moving around its enclosure during the day.

Have a **healthy appetite** and regularly consume food.

Pass normal **urine and feces**, which should be firm and consistent in shape.

Regularly observe your tortoise for any behavioral or physical changes, as early detection of health problems can lead to better outcomes.

3. Common Illnesses in Leopard Tortoises

Despite their hardiness, leopard tortoises can suffer from a variety of health problems. Being aware of common diseases and conditions will help you catch them early and get the necessary treatment.

a. Respiratory Infections

Respiratory infections are a common issue for reptiles, including leopard tortoises. These can be caused by poor enclosure conditions (particularly incorrect temperature or humidity) or bacterial infections.

- **Symptoms**: Wheezing, nasal discharge, open-mouth breathing, lethargy, or lack of appetite.
- **Treatment**: A veterinarian will often prescribe antibiotics or a humidifier to help treat respiratory infections. It is essential to address environmental factors such as temperature and humidity to prevent recurrence.

b. Metabolic Bone Disease (MBD)

MBD is a condition caused by calcium deficiency, often exacerbated by insufficient UVB light or improper dietary calcium.

- **Symptoms**: Soft, deformed shell, lethargy, difficulty moving, tremors, or seizures.
- **Treatment**: Treatment involves providing calcium supplements and increasing UVB exposure. In severe cases, a veterinarian may need to administer calcium injections.

c. Shell Rot

Shell rot is a bacterial or fungal infection that causes the shell to soften or become infected, often due to a wet, unclean environment.

- **Symptoms**: Softening of the shell, discoloration, foul smell, or visible lesions on the shell.
- **Treatment**: Treatment may involve cleaning the shell with a mild antiseptic, improving enclosure cleanliness, and using prescribed topical medications or oral antibiotics.

d. Eye Infections

Eye infections can be caused by poor environmental conditions, such as high humidity, poor ventilation, or trauma to the eyes.

Symptoms: Watery or cloudy eyes, swelling, or excessive blinking.

Treatment: Depending on the cause, eye infections can be treated with topical antibiotics, improved enclosure conditions, or adjustments to lighting.

e. Gastrointestinal Problems

Leopard tortoises can suffer from digestive issues, often related to diet or stress. Constipation is common, particularly when the tortoise is dehydrated or not eating properly.

Symptoms: Lack of feces, bloating, or lethargy.

Treatment: Ensure the tortoise has access to water at all times and offer a high-fiber diet. In some cases, a veterinarian may need to administer fluids or medications to relieve constipation.

f. Parasites

Tortoises can be susceptible to internal and external parasites, especially if they are housed in unclean environments or have been exposed to other infected animals.

Symptoms: Weight loss, lethargy, diarrhea, and visible parasites in the feces.

Treatment: A fecal test at the vet will help diagnose parasites. Treatment usually involves medication or deworming.

4. The Importance of Regular Vet Visits

Even with proper care, it's important to schedule regular veterinary visits to ensure your leopard tortoise remains in good health. Veterinarians with experience in reptile care can offer specialized advice on diet, habitat, and health concerns. Regular check-ups also help detect potential issues before they become serious.

a. Annual Check-Ups

At least once a year, take your tortoise to a reptile veterinarian for a thorough examination. This will allow for early detection of any health issues, including respiratory infections, shell issues, and nutritional deficiencies. The vet will also check for parasites and monitor the overall condition of your tortoise.

b. Routine Health Monitoring

Shell Health: Your vet will inspect the shell for any cracks, lesions, or signs of rot.

Bloodwork: Blood tests may be used to check for signs of infection, organ function, and calcium levels.

Weight Check: Monitoring weight is essential, as weight loss or sudden weight gain can be signs of illness or stress.

c. When to Seek Veterinary Care

If you notice any changes in your tortoise's behavior, appetite, or physical appearance (such as swollen eyes, abnormal shell condition, or signs of infection), seek veterinary care immediately. Early intervention is often the key to successful treatment.

Preventative care for your leopard tortoise is essential for maintaining its health and well-being. Providing a proper habitat, a balanced diet, and a clean living environment are all key factors in preventing illness. Regular veterinary visits, along with early recognition of potential health issues, will help ensure your tortoise lives a long, healthy life. Remember that your leopard tortoise depends on you for care and attention, so staying informed and proactive is crucial to being a responsible pet owner.

Recognizing and Treating Common Health Issues in Leopard Tortoises

Leopard tortoises, like all reptiles, can face a variety of health challenges. Recognizing and addressing these issues early is essential to ensuring a long and healthy life for your tortoise. In this section, we will explore some of the most common health issues that can affect leopard tortoises, the symptoms to look for, and how to treat or prevent these conditions.

1. Respiratory Infections

Respiratory infections (RI) are one of the most common health problems in reptiles, including leopard tortoises. They are typically caused by bacterial, viral, or fungal infections that are aggravated by poor environmental conditions, such as incorrect temperature, humidity, or hygiene.

Symptoms of Respiratory Infections:

- **Nasal discharge** (clear or cloudy mucus)
- **Open-mouth breathing**
- **Wheezing or crackling sounds**
- **Swollen eyes** or watery discharge
- **Lethargy** and reduced activity levels
- **Loss of appetite**

Causes:

- **Incorrect temperature**: If the enclosure is too cold or too hot, it can stress the tortoise and weaken its immune system, making it susceptible to respiratory infections.

Low humidity: Insufficient humidity can dry out the respiratory system, making it more prone to infections.

Poor ventilation: Stale air in an enclosed space can lead to respiratory distress.

Inadequate hygiene: Dirty enclosures or contaminated water sources can harbor bacteria or fungal spores that lead to infections.

Treatment:

Veterinary care: If you suspect a respiratory infection, it's essential to take your tortoise to a reptile vet. A veterinarian may administer antibiotics or antifungal treatments to combat the infection.

Improve the enclosure: Ensure that the habitat has proper temperature and humidity levels. The temperature should be kept between **75°F and 95°F** (24°C to 35°C) during the day, with cooler nighttime temperatures between **65°F and 75°F** (18°C to 24°C), and humidity levels should be between **50% and 70%**.

Provide warmth: Use a heat lamp or basking area to provide warmth, as tortoises need heat to recover from illness. A basking spot of **95°F to 100°F** (35°C to 38°C) is ideal.

Isolate the sick tortoise: If possible, isolate the infected tortoise to prevent the spread of any potential contagious infections.

2. Metabolic Bone Disease (MBD)

Metabolic Bone Disease (MBD) is a common health issue among captive reptiles and is often linked to improper calcium intake or insufficient UVB lighting. MBD causes soft, deformed bones and shell, as well as muscle weakness.

Symptoms of MBD:

Soft, deformed shell (shell appears pliable or swollen)

Lethargy and lack of movement

Difficulty walking or standing

Tremors or twitching

Decreased appetite

Swollen limbs or facial bones

Causes:

Calcium deficiency: An inadequate supply of calcium in the diet is one of the leading causes of MBD. Tortoises need a calcium-rich diet, and calcium is vital for the development and maintenance of strong bones and shells.

Lack of UVB lighting: UVB light helps reptiles synthesize vitamin D3, which is necessary for the absorption of calcium. Without adequate UVB exposure, calcium cannot be properly absorbed, leading to MBD.

Improper diet: A diet high in phosphorus (such as too much fruit or high-protein foods) and low in calcium can contribute to MBD.

Treatment:

Calcium supplementation: Start supplementing the tortoise's diet with calcium powder. Offer a high-calcium diet, such as leafy greens like collard greens, dandelion, and mustard greens. You can also provide cuttlebone or calcium blocks for your tortoise to gnaw on.

Increase UVB exposure: Ensure that your tortoise has access to appropriate UVB lighting for **10 to 12 hours a day** if kept indoors. If possible, allow the tortoise to get natural sunlight by placing it outside for short periods, ensuring it is safe from predators and extreme temperatures.

Veterinary treatment: In severe cases of MBD, a vet may provide calcium injections or other treatments. Prompt intervention is crucial to prevent permanent damage to the bones or shell.

3. Shell Rot

Shell rot is a fungal or bacterial infection that causes the shell to deteriorate, becoming soft, discolored, or developing foul-smelling lesions. This condition is often caused by poor environmental hygiene or excessive moisture.

Symptoms of Shell Rot:

Discoloration or **dark spots** on the shell

Softening or **mushy patches** on the shell

Foul smell emanating from the shell

Visible lesions or open sores

Swelling around the affected areas

Causes:

Excessive moisture: Keeping the tortoise in a humid or wet environment can cause the shell to soften and become susceptible to bacterial or fungal infections.

Dirty living conditions: A dirty enclosure with unclean bedding, water, or food can harbor bacteria and fungi that infect the shell.

Trauma to the shell: Any physical injury, such as a fall or rough handling, can allow bacteria or fungi to enter and infect the shell.

Treatment:

Clean the shell: If you notice signs of shell rot, gently clean the affected area with a diluted antiseptic solution (such as iodine or betadine) to disinfect it. Be sure to follow the instructions carefully, as improper cleaning can further irritate the tortoise.

Dry the shell: Allow the tortoise to dry out for a few days in a clean, dry environment. This helps prevent further fungal or bacterial growth.

Veterinary care: If the infection is severe, consult a veterinarian. The vet may need to remove damaged shell tissue or prescribe antibiotics to treat the infection. In some cases, topical antifungal or antibacterial treatments may be required.

4. Gastrointestinal Problems

Leopard tortoises can experience digestive issues, which may include constipation, diarrhea, or bloating. These problems are often related to diet, hydration, or stress.

Symptoms of Gastrointestinal Issues:

Diarrhea or **loose stool**

Constipation or difficulty passing stool

Bloating or swelling of the abdomen

Lethargy or reduced movement

Refusal to eat or decreased appetite

Causes:

Dehydration: Tortoises need constant access to fresh water to stay hydrated. Dehydration can lead to constipation or digestive problems.

Improper diet: A diet low in fiber or too high in protein or fruits can lead to digestive issues. Too much fruit, in particular, can cause diarrhea.

Stress: Environmental stressors such as changes in temperature, humidity, or handling can affect the tortoise's digestive system.

Treatment:

Hydration: Offer plenty of fresh water and consider providing a shallow water dish large enough for the tortoise to soak in. This can help with dehydration and constipation.

Adjust the diet: Offer more fiber-rich foods like leafy greens and grasses. Avoid high-protein foods and excessive fruits. Ensure that the diet is well-balanced.

Veterinary care: If the problem persists or if there are signs of serious illness, seek veterinary assistance. The vet may prescribe medications or provide fluids for hydration.

5. Eye Infections

Eye infections in leopard tortoises are common, especially if they are housed in an environment with improper humidity, poor hygiene, or inadequate UVB lighting.

Symptoms of Eye Infections:

Watery eyes or **cloudy discharge**

Swollen or red eyes

Excessive blinking or squinting

Bulging eyes

Refusal to eat

Causes:

Low humidity: If the air is too dry, the tortoise's eyes can become irritated, leading to infection.

Poor enclosure hygiene: Dirty bedding or water can introduce bacteria and other pathogens that affect the eyes.

Lack of UVB lighting: Insufficient UVB exposure can lead to eye problems and weaken the tortoise's immune system.

Treatment:

- **Increase humidity**: Ensure that the enclosure maintains proper humidity levels, which can help prevent eye dryness and irritation.
- **Clean the eyes**: Gently wipe the eyes with a damp cotton swab soaked in saline solution to remove any discharge.
- **Veterinary care**: If the infection persists or if the eye is swollen or severely infected, a veterinarian may prescribe eye drops or antibiotics.

Preventing and recognizing health issues in leopard tortoises requires attentiveness to their environmental conditions, diet, and overall care. Ensuring that your tortoise has a clean, well-maintained enclosure, a balanced diet, proper lighting, and regular health check-ups can significantly reduce the risk of illness. If you observe any symptoms of illness, it is crucial to seek veterinary assistance promptly to ensure that your tortoise receives the best possible care. By staying proactive in maintaining your tortoise's health, you can help ensure a long and healthy life for your companion.

Chapter Seven

Breeding Leopard Tortoises in Captivity: Breeding Season and Care for Hatchlings

Breeding leopard tortoises in captivity can be a rewarding experience for dedicated tortoise keepers, but it requires careful planning, attention to detail, and an understanding of the natural reproductive cycle of these tortoises. The breeding season, care of the adult tortoises, and the proper rearing of hatchlings all play critical roles in the success of captive breeding. This section will guide you through the key aspects of breeding leopard tortoises and the specific care needed for hatchlings.

1. Breeding Season of Leopard Tortoises

Leopard tortoises (Stigmochelys pardalis) are typically seasonal breeders. In the wild, their breeding season is influenced by environmental factors such as temperature, humidity, and food availability, often corresponding to the wet season. In captivity, you can mimic these natural conditions to encourage successful breeding.

a. Timing of Breeding

The breeding season for leopard tortoises generally takes place during the **warmer months**, usually between **spring and early fall** (April to September). During this time, female tortoises become receptive to mating. However, they can breed year-round if conditions (such as temperature, light, and humidity) are controlled appropriately in captivity.

b. Mating Behavior

Male leopard tortoises will exhibit certain behaviors to court females. This includes:

- **Ramming or butting the female's shell** with their heads or front legs.
- **Vocalizations**: Males may make loud "screeching" noises during courtship, which is often heard when a male is trying to impress a female.
- **Chasing**: The male may chase the female, showing persistence in his attempts to mate. Mating can last several hours, and

once copulation is successful, the female may store sperm and fertilize eggs over several weeks before laying them.

2. Preparing for Breeding

Before attempting to breed leopard tortoises, it is crucial to create the proper conditions that encourage mating and ensure the health of both males and females.

a. Age and Size of Breeding Tortoises

- **Maturity**: Leopard tortoises generally reach sexual maturity at around **5 to 7 years** of age, though this can vary depending on diet, habitat, and overall health.
- **Size**: Female tortoises are usually larger than males and have a broader, flatter shell. Ensure that the female is healthy and fully mature before breeding.
- **Health**: Both the male and female must be in optimal health to ensure a successful breeding process. This includes a proper diet, UVB exposure, hydration, and an appropriate temperature range.

b. Environmental Conditions

To simulate the breeding season, ensure the following:

Temperature: The temperature should be warm, ideally between **75°F to 95°F** (24°C to 35°C) during the day, with a **basking spot** around **95°F to 100°F** (35°C to 38°C). Nighttime temperatures can drop to **65°F to 75°F** (18°C to 24°C).

Lighting and UVB: UVB lighting is essential for proper calcium metabolism and egg production in females. Tortoises require **10 to 12 hours of UVB exposure** each day to simulate natural daylight hours.

Humidity: Ensure a **humidity level of 50% to 70%**, as low humidity can cause reproductive issues, particularly with egg development.

c. Creating a Safe and Comfortable Nesting Area

Females require a **nesting site** in which to lay their eggs. This should be:

A spacious, soft substrate: Provide a mixture of **soil, sand, and coconut coir** in a nesting box or an outdoor enclosure to allow the female to dig.

Space to roam: Ensure that the enclosure is large enough for the female to roam freely, as they tend to dig burrows to lay their eggs.

Temperature and humidity: Maintain proper warmth and humidity in the nesting area to encourage egg development.

3. Egg Laying Process

Once copulation occurs, the female leopard tortoise will begin preparing to lay her eggs. She typically does so several weeks after mating, and the process involves the following steps:

a. Preparing the Nest

The female will dig a hole in the nesting area, usually about **6 to 8 inches** deep, and begin depositing her eggs. Leopard tortoises can lay anywhere from **6 to 12 eggs** in a single clutch, though the exact number varies. The female will carefully cover the eggs with soil to protect them from the environment.

b. Egg Incubation

Once the female has laid her eggs, they will need to be incubated to ensure successful hatching. The following conditions are ideal for incubating leopard tortoise eggs:

Temperature: The eggs should be incubated at a **temperature of 85°F to 88°F** (29°C to 31°C). Higher temperatures can cause premature hatching, while lower temperatures can slow development.

Humidity: Maintain a humidity level of around **60% to 80%** during incubation. Too little humidity can lead to shriveled eggs, while too much can cause mold or rot.

Incubation Duration: Leopard tortoise eggs generally take between **90 to 120 days** to hatch, depending on environmental conditions such as temperature and humidity.

c. Incubators

If you are incubating the eggs indoors, use a reliable **incubator** that maintains stable temperature and humidity levels. It is important to monitor the eggs closely and adjust the incubator settings as necessary to ensure optimal conditions.

4. Care for Hatchlings

Once the eggs have hatched, it's important to provide proper care for the hatchlings to ensure they grow into healthy juveniles.

a. Hatchling Characteristics

Newly hatched leopard tortoises are typically about **2 to 3 inches** long and will have a slightly soft shell, which will harden as they mature. Hatchlings may be more vulnerable to illness and environmental stresses, so special care is needed during this early stage.

b. Housing and Temperature

Small Enclosure: Hatchlings should be housed in a small, secure enclosure that prevents them from escaping. It should be spacious enough for them to roam but not so large that they become stressed.

Temperature: Keep the enclosure at **80°F to 85°F** (27°C to 29°C) during the day, with a basking spot at **90°F to 95°F** (32°C to 35°C). At night, temperatures can drop to **70°F to 75°F** (21°C to 24°C).

Humidity: Maintain humidity around **50% to 60%** to prevent dehydration and encourage healthy shell growth.

c. Diet and Nutrition

Leafy Greens: Offer a diet rich in **dark leafy greens** such as **collard greens, mustard greens**, and **dandelion greens**. Hatchlings need a calcium-rich diet to ensure proper bone and shell development.

Water: Provide fresh water in a shallow dish that the hatchlings can easily access. Regular hydration is crucial for their growth and health.

Calcium Supplements: Dust the food with a calcium supplement to promote healthy shell development. Make sure the hatchlings also have access to UVB lighting or natural sunlight to help with calcium absorption.

d. Socialization and Handling

Avoid handling hatchlings excessively, as this can cause stress. Instead, focus on providing a stable, secure environment where they can grow and acclimate. Over time, as they mature, you can introduce handling sessions to help them become more accustomed to human interaction.

5. Monitoring Growth and Health

Regularly monitor the health and growth of hatchlings. Key areas to check include:

- **Shell growth**: The shell should grow evenly and maintain a smooth texture. Any deformities or soft spots may indicate health issues.
- **Activity levels**: Hatchlings should be active, exploring their environment, and eating well. Lethargy or loss of appetite can be signs of illness or stress.
- **Weight**: Ensure the hatchlings are gaining weight appropriately. Stunted growth or weight loss may indicate health concerns or an inadequate diet.

Breeding leopard tortoises in captivity requires careful planning, attention to environmental conditions, and proper care for both adults and hatchlings. By mimicking their natural breeding cycle, creating the right habitat, and providing the necessary care, you can ensure that your tortoises reproduce successfully and that the hatchlings thrive into healthy juveniles. Always prioritize the well-being of the tortoises, and be prepared for the responsibility that comes with breeding, including the potential need to find suitable homes for the offspring once they have grown.

Remember that breeding should only be undertaken by experienced tortoise keepers who are committed to the welfare of the animals involved.

Incubation and Egg Care for Leopard Tortoises

Incubating leopard tortoise eggs is a crucial process for ensuring the successful hatching of healthy offspring. Both the environment and the care provided to the eggs during incubation play a critical role in the development of the embryos inside. This section will detail the steps required for proper egg care, including how to handle, incubate, and monitor the eggs until they hatch.

1. Preparing for Egg Incubation

Before you begin the incubation process, there are several steps you should take to ensure that the environment is ideal for the developing eggs.

a. Collecting the Eggs

Once the female leopard tortoise has laid her eggs, it's important to handle them gently to avoid damaging them. Here are the steps to follow:

- **Timing**: Eggs should be collected **immediately after laying** to prevent any environmental factors (like changes in temperature or humidity) from affecting them. If the eggs are left in the nesting site for too long, they could become vulnerable to contamination or pests.
- **Do not rotate the eggs**: When collecting the eggs, avoid rotating them. Tortoise eggs are typically laid in a specific orientation, and turning them may damage the embryos inside.
- **Clean the eggs carefully**: If the eggs have any dirt or debris on them, gently wipe them with a soft, damp cloth to clean

them. Be careful not to remove any part of the shell, as it acts as a protective barrier for the developing embryo.

b. Identifying the Right Incubator

The key to successful incubation is using the right incubator, which will control temperature, humidity, and ventilation.

- **Incubator type**: Use a **reliable reptile egg incubator** that maintains stable temperature and humidity levels. There are also homemade incubators you can build, but they must have a regulated heat source and be able to maintain consistent conditions.
- **Incubator substrate**: Prepare the incubator by adding an appropriate substrate to support the eggs. You can use materials such as **vermiculite, perlite**, or **coconut coir**. These substrates hold moisture and provide a stable environment for the eggs.
- **Egg positioning**: Place the eggs gently on the substrate, keeping them in the same orientation as when they were laid. Ensure that they are not crowded together and have some space for air circulation.

2. Temperature and Humidity for Incubation

The temperature and humidity levels during incubation must be closely monitored to ensure the embryos develop properly.

a. Temperature

Leopard tortoise eggs require a specific temperature range for proper development.

- **Ideal incubation temperature**: The best temperature range for incubating leopard tortoise eggs is **85°F to 88°F** (29°C to 31°C).
- **Variation**: Some slight fluctuation in temperature is acceptable but should not exceed a range of **82°F to 90°F** (28°C to 32°C). Consistent temperatures are important because fluctuations can lead to developmental issues or even embryo death.
- **Temperature extremes**: If the temperature exceeds **90°F** (32°C), it can lead to early hatching or deformities. Temperatures below **80°F** (27°C) can slow the embryos' development or result in death.

b. Humidity

Humidity plays an essential role in egg development and hatching. Too much moisture can cause the eggs to rot, while too little moisture can lead to shriveled or dehydrated eggs.

Ideal humidity: The incubation humidity should be maintained between **60% to 80%**. This allows the eggs to retain enough moisture for the embryos to develop while preventing excessive moisture that can lead to bacterial or fungal growth.

Humidity monitoring: Use a **hygrometer** to monitor the humidity levels inside the incubator. If necessary, mist the eggs gently with water to raise humidity. However, avoid directly soaking the eggs, as this can promote mold growth or drowning of the embryos.

c. Air circulation

Proper airflow is essential for the developing embryos to get oxygen. Ensure that the incubator has adequate ventilation but not enough to cause fluctuations in temperature or humidity.

3. Monitoring the Eggs

Regular monitoring of the eggs is essential to ensure that conditions remain stable and that no issues arise during the incubation process.

a. Checking for Mold and Fungus

Mold and fungal growth are common problems during egg incubation, especially if humidity is too high or if the eggs are not properly ventilated.

Preventing mold: To prevent mold growth, make sure the substrate is not too wet. If you see mold forming on the eggs, carefully remove the affected eggs and clean them with a diluted antiseptic solution (such as iodine or a weak bleach solution). Always ensure the eggs dry out fully before returning them to the incubator.

Humidity control: Maintaining proper humidity levels is crucial. If the substrate becomes too wet, it can create a breeding ground for mold, while very dry conditions can cause the eggs to dry out and dehydrate.

b. Turning the Eggs

While it's important not to rotate the eggs after collection, you may need to **gently turn the eggs once a week** during incubation to simulate the natural process in the wild. This can help prevent the developing embryo from sticking to the eggshell, but be very careful and handle the eggs delicately.

Marking the eggs: You can mark the eggs lightly with a pencil to identify the top side and avoid turning them incorrectly.

Only turn the eggs one-quarter of a turn in each direction, and always return them to their original orientation.

c. Candling the Eggs

Candling involves shining a light through the eggs to check on the progress of the embryos inside. This can be done around **30 to 40 days** into the incubation process.

- **Candling procedure**: Use a flashlight or candling lamp to gently illuminate the egg. In a dark room, you should be able to see the developing embryo and the progression of blood vessels. This will allow you to assess the health of the embryo and identify any potential issues.
- **Signs of a healthy embryo**: A healthy embryo will show a visible network of blood vessels, and you may be able to see slight movement inside the egg.
- **Dead embryos**: If there is no visible movement and the egg appears to be opaque or the embryo has stopped developing, it may indicate that the egg is no longer viable.

4. Hatching the Eggs

As the eggs approach the end of the incubation period (around **90 to 120 days**), the embryos will begin to prepare for hatching. Here's how to handle the hatching process.

a. Hatching Time

Signs of hatching: The eggs will begin to show signs of hatching when small cracks appear in the shell, typically a few days before the hatchling breaks free. At this point, the hatchlings are ready to emerge, and it is important to resist the urge to intervene.

The hatchling's process: Leopard tortoises may take several hours to completely emerge from their eggs. They use an egg tooth (a temporary structure on the snout) to break open the shell.

b. Do not assist: It's important not to assist the hatchlings in breaking out of the shell, as doing so may cause injury or stress. Allow the hatchlings to emerge naturally. If the hatchling appears stuck or unable to break free after a prolonged period, consult a veterinarian for guidance.

5. Post-Hatching Care

After the hatchlings emerge from their eggs, they require careful care to ensure they grow into healthy juveniles.

a. Remove the hatchlings

Once hatched, remove the hatchlings from the incubator and place them in a **separate enclosure** that is designed for young tortoises. The enclosure should include:

Appropriate heating: Maintain a basking area at **90°F to 95°F** (32°C to 35°C) and overall ambient temperatures of around **80°F to 85°F** (27°C to 29°C).

Humidity: Keep the humidity at around **50% to 60%** to ensure the hatchlings do not become dehydrated.

b. Hydration and Food

First meals: Hatchlings typically do not eat immediately after hatching. Allow them to rest for a day or two to recover from the hatching process before offering food.

Diet: Offer a variety of **leafy greens** (such as dandelion, collard greens, and mustard greens) along with access to fresh water.

Calcium supplements: Ensure that hatchlings have access to a calcium-rich diet and offer appropriate calcium supplementation.

c. UVB Lighting

Like adult leopard tortoises, hatchlings require UVB lighting to help them process calcium properly and grow strong bones and shells. Provide **10 to 12 hours** of UVB exposure each day.

Incubating leopard tortoise eggs successfully requires attention to detail, proper environmental conditions, and patience. By maintaining the correct temperature, humidity, and providing gentle care during the incubation period, you can ensure the healthy development of embryos and the successful hatching of your leopard tortoises. Post-hatching care is just as important, and with the right environment, diet, and monitoring, your hatchlings can grow into healthy juveniles ready to thrive in their new homes.

Chapter Eight

Leopard Tortoise Lifespan and Aging: How Long Do Leopard Tortoises Live?

Leopard tortoises (Stigmochelys pardalis) are known for their remarkable longevity, making them a popular choice for reptile enthusiasts who are ready to commit to the long-term care of these gentle creatures. Understanding the lifespan and aging process of leopard tortoises is important for providing proper care and ensuring a healthy life for these fascinating animals.

1. Average Lifespan of Leopard Tortoises

Leopard tortoises are among the longest-lived tortoise species. In both the wild and in captivity, their lifespan can vary based on a range of factors such as diet, living conditions, and overall health.

a. In the Wild

In the wild, leopard tortoises can live anywhere from **50 to 80 years**, depending on environmental conditions, food availability, and the presence of predators. While they may face challenges such as predation, extreme weather, or lack of food, their natural instincts and survival skills allow them to thrive for several decades.

b. In Captivity

When properly cared for in captivity, leopard tortoises tend to live a bit longer than their wild counterparts, with many reaching an impressive age of **70 to 100 years**. However, some individuals have been known to live beyond this, with reports of some living up to **120 years** or more. The key to a long life for a leopard tortoise in captivity includes a suitable habitat, balanced diet, regular veterinary care, and attention to their specific needs.

2. Factors Affecting Leopard Tortoise Lifespan

Several factors influence the lifespan of a leopard tortoise. These factors can either help extend their lives or cause them to experience health problems that shorten their life expectancy.

a. Diet and Nutrition

A proper diet is one of the most important factors in ensuring the longevity of a leopard tortoise. Poor nutrition can lead to serious health issues such as metabolic bone disease, shell deformities, or kidney problems, all of which can negatively impact lifespan.

High-fiber, low-protein diet: Leopard tortoises thrive on a diet that is rich in high-fiber plants like grasses, hay, and leafy greens. Avoid high-protein foods like lettuce, as these can cause digestive and metabolic problems.

Calcium and Vitamin D: Calcium is crucial for maintaining a strong shell and healthy bones. Leopard tortoises also need UVB light exposure to process calcium effectively, either from natural sunlight or artificial UVB lighting.

Hydration: Keeping your tortoise well-hydrated by providing fresh water is important for its overall health. Dehydration can lead to kidney failure, which can reduce lifespan.

b. Habitat Conditions

Leopard tortoises need an environment that closely mimics their natural habitat to live a long, healthy life.

Temperature: Leopard tortoises are cold-blooded and need a warm environment to thrive. They require a basking area with temperatures between **95°F to 100°F** (35°C to 38°C) and an ambient temperature of **75°F to 85°F** (24°C to 29°C). Nighttime temperatures should be cooler but not drop below **60°F** (16°C).

UVB Lighting: UVB rays are essential for tortoises to synthesize vitamin D3, which helps them absorb calcium from their food. Providing UVB light for **10 to 12 hours a day** is essential for their long-term health and longevity.

Space: Leopard tortoises need plenty of space to roam and exercise. Overcrowded enclosures can cause stress, leading to health problems that may shorten their lifespan. An outdoor enclosure with plenty of access to natural sunlight and vegetation is ideal.

c. Veterinary Care

Regular checkups with a veterinarian experienced in reptile care are important for monitoring a leopard tortoise's health. Regular exams can catch health issues early, and a vet can provide preventive care such as vaccinations and parasite control.

Parasite control: Leopard tortoises are susceptible to various parasites, such as ticks, mites, and internal worms. Keeping them parasite-free is essential for maintaining their health and lifespan.

Shell health: The tortoise's shell is a vital part of its body, and it's important to prevent shell rot and other conditions that can arise from injury or poor care.

d. Genetics

The genetics of a leopard tortoise also play a role in its lifespan. Just like in other species, some tortoises may be genetically predisposed to certain health issues or may have stronger resilience to environmental stressors. While you can't change the genetics, proper care can help maximize the potential lifespan of a tortoise.

3. Aging Process in Leopard Tortoises

Understanding how leopard tortoises age is important for providing them with appropriate care throughout their lifespan. Their aging process is gradual, and they show signs of aging as they reach their later years.

a. Growth and Development

Leopard tortoises grow steadily in their younger years and can reach maturity around **5 to 7 years** of age. The growth rate can be influenced by factors like diet, habitat, and genetics.

- **Juvenile growth**: In the first few years of life, leopard tortoises will grow rapidly, and their shell will become harder and more developed.
- **Mature tortoises**: Once they reach adulthood, their growth slows significantly. At this stage, the size of the tortoise will stabilize, and the shell will become more solid and rounded.

b. Physical Changes with Age

As leopard tortoises get older, they may experience a few physical changes:

Slower metabolism: Older tortoises tend to have a slower metabolism, which can result in a decreased appetite and less activity.

Shell wear and tear: Over time, a tortoise's shell may show signs of wear. While tortoises' shells are incredibly durable, the outer scutes (the hard plates on the shell) can become worn down over the years. Old age can also result in a slightly thinner shell, which is not necessarily a sign of illness but should be monitored.

Reduced mobility: In some cases, elderly leopard tortoises may become less mobile due to joint stiffness or health problems, which can limit their ability to forage or explore.

c. Signs of Old Age

Reduced activity levels: Older leopard tortoises often become less active, and they may spend more time resting or basking.

Health problems: As tortoises age, they may develop certain health issues, including arthritis, poor eyesight, or digestive problems. Regular checkups and proper care can help manage these conditions.

Weight loss: Elderly tortoises may lose weight, especially if they are not eating as much. This can be a natural part of the aging process, but it can also signal an underlying health issue that should be addressed by a veterinarian.

4. Extending the Lifespan of Your Leopard Tortoise

While leopard tortoises naturally live a long time, there are several ways you can help ensure that your tortoise enjoys a long and healthy life:

a. Proper Nutrition

As discussed earlier, providing a proper diet is one of the most important factors in maintaining the health and longevity of your tortoise. Be sure to provide a variety of high-quality, fibrous plants and ensure they have access to calcium-rich foods and proper UVB exposure.

b. Stress Reduction

Stress is one of the most detrimental factors to a tortoise's health. Providing a stable, quiet environment, avoiding excessive handling, and ensuring they have enough space to roam can help reduce stress and prevent health problems related to it.

c. Regular Vet Checkups

Regular veterinary visits are essential for monitoring your tortoise's health, especially as they age. A vet can detect early signs of disease, nutritional imbalances, or parasites, allowing for prompt treatment and improving the chances of a long life.

d. Enclosure Care

Ensure that your tortoise's enclosure is clean, safe, and properly maintained. Regularly clean the enclosure and check for any hazards that could injure your tortoise.

Leopard tortoises are long-lived reptiles, with lifespans ranging from 50 to 100 years or more, depending on various factors such as diet, habitat, and overall care. By providing the proper environment, diet, and regular veterinary care, you can help ensure that your leopard tortoise lives a long, healthy life. Understanding the aging process and how to address the unique needs of older tortoises will help you enjoy many years with your pet, and in some cases, decades of companionship. With the right care, a leopard tortoise can become a part of your family for a lifetime.

Signs of Aging and Adjustments in Care for Leopard Tortoises

As leopard tortoises age, they undergo various physical and behavioral changes. Recognizing these signs of aging and adjusting their care accordingly is essential to ensure that they remain comfortable and healthy in their later years. Like all long-lived reptiles, leopard tortoises may experience changes in their mobility, diet, and general health as they mature. This section will guide you through the signs of aging in leopard tortoises and the adjustments you can make in their care to ensure they continue to thrive well into old age.

1. Physical Signs of Aging

Leopard tortoises, like most reptiles, exhibit certain physical changes as they age. These changes are often gradual but can significantly affect their behavior, health, and overall well-being.

a. Decreased Growth Rate

Growth stabilization: One of the first signs of aging in a leopard tortoise is a decreased rate of growth. During their early years, leopard tortoises grow rapidly, reaching full size between **10 to 15 years** of age. After reaching maturity, their growth slows significantly, and they may stop growing altogether.

Smaller size and less shell growth: Older tortoises tend to have more stable shell sizes, with fewer changes or growth spurts. The shell may become slightly worn and smoother with age.

b. Changes in Shell Appearance

Shell wear: As leopard tortoises age, the outer scutes (the hard, keratinized plates on the shell) may show signs of wear. While tortoise shells are durable, they can experience gradual thinning over time due to years of use. The wear may be more visible in older tortoises that have lived in environments with varying temperatures and conditions.

Slight thinning of the shell: It's not uncommon for older tortoises to have a slightly thinner shell, but this should be monitored carefully. Thin spots or cracks could indicate an underlying health issue, such as calcium deficiency or shell rot. Regular veterinary checkups can help identify potential problems early.

Age-related deformities: Some older tortoises may develop shell deformities due to years of environmental stress or metabolic issues, such as pyramiding (the raised, pyramid-like growth of the scutes). While pyramiding often occurs in younger tortoises due to improper care, it may become more apparent with age.

c. Reduced Mobility

Slower movements: As leopard tortoises age, their mobility tends to decrease. Older tortoises often move more slowly, with less energy and stamina than younger ones. This is primarily due to the natural aging process and possible arthritis or joint stiffness that comes with age.

Less climbing or digging: Older tortoises may show less interest in climbing or digging, which are typical behaviors of younger tortoises in the wild. While some reduction in activity is natural, if mobility significantly decreases, it could signal health problems, such as arthritis or metabolic bone disease.

Stiffness and joint pain: As tortoises age, they can develop arthritis or other joint issues, which can cause stiffness, difficulty walking, and reluctance to move. This can be particularly noticeable when they attempt to climb or walk on hard surfaces.

d. Decreased Activity and Resting Behavior

Longer periods of rest: Older tortoises may sleep or rest for longer periods of time. While younger tortoises are often active and curious, older tortoises are more likely to spend the majority of their time resting in one spot or basking in a warm area.

Less foraging: With aging, tortoises may show less interest in foraging for food. A lack of enthusiasm for searching for food could be due to a slower metabolism, aging joints, or the overall decline in activity levels.

2. Behavioral Changes with Age

As leopard tortoises age, they may exhibit a number of behavioral changes that reflect their reduced energy levels, sensory function, and overall health.

a. Reduced Appetite

Changes in appetite: A decrease in appetite is a common sign of aging in tortoises. Older tortoises may eat less, particularly if they have slowed metabolism, dental problems, or arthritis that makes eating less comfortable.

Selective feeding: Some older tortoises may become more selective about the types of food they eat, preferring specific greens or food textures. This is normal, but it may also indicate that they are having difficulty eating certain foods due to changes in their jaws or mouth, possibly caused by wear over time.

Weight loss: If a tortoise consistently eats less, it may begin to lose weight. While slight weight loss is typical in elderly tortoises, significant weight loss is a red flag and should be addressed by a veterinarian to rule out underlying health issues such as malnutrition, parasites, or organ failure.

b. Decreased Socialization

Less interaction: Older tortoises may become less interested in interacting with humans or other tortoises. They may prefer to spend more time alone in a comfortable, quiet area.

Behavioral changes due to reduced energy: As their energy levels decrease, older tortoises may not engage as much in behaviors like exploring, mating, or basking. Instead, they may prefer to stay in one location for long periods, especially during the cooler parts of the day.

3. Adjustments in Care for Aging Leopard Tortoises

To ensure that your leopard tortoise remains healthy and comfortable as it ages, it's important to make certain adjustments in its care routine. These adjustments can help alleviate the physical and behavioral changes associated with aging.

a. Provide More Comfortable and Accessible Housing

Soft, cushioned bedding: As tortoises age and become less mobile, it is beneficial to provide soft bedding that supports their joints. Materials like **coconut coir**, **paper-based bedding**, or **sphagnum moss** can provide cushioning for their sensitive shells and joints. Make sure the bedding is dry to prevent bacterial or fungal growth.

Accessible ramps or surfaces: If your tortoise has difficulty climbing or walking, consider adding ramps or smooth, low surfaces to help them get around their enclosure without straining themselves.

Separate enclosure or resting area: Older tortoises may prefer a quieter space where they can rest undisturbed. Provide a separate, cozy area within the enclosure where the tortoise can retreat if it becomes overwhelmed or prefers solitude.

b. Adjust Temperature and Lighting

Ensure proper heat and lighting: Older tortoises still need access to warmth and UVB light to maintain good health, but they may be more sensitive to temperature extremes. Ensure that their basking area is maintained at a consistent temperature of **95°F to 100°F** (35°C to 38°C) and that they continue to receive **12 hours of UVB light** daily.

Gradual temperature shifts: Since older tortoises may have a harder time thermoregulating, avoid sudden temperature fluctuations. Keep the temperature in their enclosure steady and avoid placing them in areas that are too cold or too hot.

c. Offer a More Manageable Diet

Easier-to-digest food: As they age, some tortoises may find it harder to chew tougher foods. You can offer softer greens or pre-chopped vegetables to make it easier for them to eat. Ensure that the food is high in fiber and low in protein to mimic their natural diet.

Supplementation: Older tortoises may need additional supplementation to maintain healthy bones and shells. Calcium supplements, along with vitamin D3, are particularly important for senior tortoises who might not be processing these nutrients as efficiently. Consult your veterinarian about appropriate supplements and dosages.

Hydration: Older tortoises may become more prone to dehydration. Ensure they always have access to fresh water, and consider soaking them in shallow, lukewarm water a few times a week to help with hydration.

d. Veterinary Care and Monitoring

Regular vet visits: Older tortoises should have regular checkups with a reptile vet to monitor their overall health. This includes checking for signs of metabolic bone disease, kidney issues, or other age-related diseases. Regular checkups can help catch any potential health issues early and improve the chances of a longer, healthier life.

Joint care: If arthritis or joint stiffness becomes an issue, ask your vet about possible treatments such as pain relief medications, joint supplements, or physical therapy. Providing ramps and softer surfaces can also help alleviate joint strain.

e. Pain Management and Comfort

Pain management: Older tortoises may experience discomfort from conditions like arthritis or other age-related ailments. Speak with your vet about safe pain management options, such as mild anti-inflammatory medications, which can help your tortoise stay active and comfortable.

Comfortable resting spots: Make sure your tortoise has plenty of soft resting areas and is able to access food, water, and basking areas without difficulty. This will help reduce stress and support their quality of life.

As leopard tortoises age, they undergo several physical and behavioral changes that require adjustments in their care routine. Recognizing signs such as reduced appetite, slower movements, and decreased activity is key to understanding when your tortoise is entering its senior years. By adjusting their environment, diet, and care practices accordingly, you can ensure that your elderly tortoise remains healthy, comfortable, and happy for many more years. Providing extra care and attention as your tortoise ages will help you extend its life and allow you to enjoy the companionship of this remarkable animal for decades to come.

Chapter Nine

Leopard Tortoise Behavior and Enrichment

Leopard tortoises, native to sub-Saharan Africa, are not only remarkable for their striking appearance but also for their fascinating natural instincts and behaviors. Like all animals, they require both mental and physical stimulation to thrive in captivity. Understanding these needs and providing appropriate enrichment is essential for their well-being. This section will explore the natural instincts of leopard tortoises, how to interpret their behavior, and ways to provide enriching activities that cater to both their mental and physical needs.

1. Understanding Natural Instincts of Leopard Tortoises

Leopard tortoises, like most wild animals, have behaviors shaped by their natural environment. Understanding these behaviors will help you create a more enriching and satisfying habitat for your pet tortoise.

a. Grazing and Foraging Instincts

Grazing behavior: In the wild, leopard tortoises spend much of their day foraging for food, especially grasses and other vegetation. They are herbivores and have evolved to graze on a variety of plants, including grasses, succulents, and low shrubs. This behavior is not just for sustenance, but also part of their natural instincts to stay active and explore their environment.

Foraging for food: Leopard tortoises are known to graze for long hours, moving slowly over vast areas to find food. In captivity, it's important to provide a variety of fresh vegetation and allow the tortoise to "hunt" for their food, mimicking the natural foraging process. Scatter food around their enclosure or hide it in different areas to stimulate their natural instincts and encourage exploration.

b. Basking Behavior

Sunbasking: Leopard tortoises are ectothermic (cold-blooded) animals that rely on external heat sources to regulate their body temperature. In the wild, they spend a significant amount of time basking in the sun, absorbing UV rays to help synthesize vitamin D3, which is essential for calcium absorption.

Seeking warmth: In captivity, leopard tortoises still need opportunities to bask, either under a heat lamp or in an outdoor enclosure with access to natural sunlight. Providing a basking spot with the right temperature (around **95°F to 100°F** or **35°C to 38°C**) is essential for their health and well-being.

c. Shell Defense and Retreating

Self-defense: Leopard tortoises are equipped with a hard, protective shell that they use for defense against predators in the wild. When feeling threatened, they will retreat into their shells to protect themselves. This instinctual behavior is something that your tortoise will still display in captivity if it feels unsafe or startled.

Seeking shelter: Even in a safe, secure environment, tortoises often seek out sheltered areas in their enclosures to rest, sleep, or escape perceived threats. Providing hiding spots in their enclosure, such as logs, rocks, or plant cover, can help satisfy this instinct and give them a sense of security.

d. Territorial Behavior

Space and territory: Leopard tortoises are generally solitary creatures in the wild, and they may show signs of territoriality, especially in overcrowded enclosures. In the wild, each tortoise establishes its own area and tends to stay within it. In captivity, providing enough space for each tortoise to claim its own territory will reduce stress and prevent aggression.

Avoiding confrontation: Although leopard tortoises are not typically aggressive, they may engage in confrontational behavior if space is limited or they feel threatened. Providing separate spaces for multiple tortoises can help minimize territorial disputes and encourage a peaceful environment.

2. Providing Mental and Physical Stimulation

Just like other intelligent creatures, leopard tortoises require both mental and physical stimulation to stay healthy and happy. Enrichment activities mimic aspects of their natural behaviors, helping prevent boredom and stress.

a. Physical Stimulation: Encouraging Movement and Exploration

Large, spacious enclosures: Leopard tortoises are known for their ability to roam vast areas in the wild, and in captivity, they benefit from having ample space to explore. Enclosures should be large enough to allow the tortoise to move around freely and engage in natural behaviors such as foraging, exploring, and basking. A larger enclosure will also reduce stress by giving the tortoise more freedom to move and find shelter.

Outdoor enclosures: If possible, providing an outdoor enclosure can enhance the physical activity of your tortoise. Access to natural sunlight allows them to bask and engage in more dynamic behaviors like digging or searching for food. Outdoor enclosures with natural grass, rocks, and safe plants allow the tortoise to indulge in instincts like grazing, burrowing, and exploring.

Climbing structures and obstacles: While leopard tortoises don't climb in the same way some species do, they will still enjoy the opportunity to explore varied terrains. Include small rocks, logs, or low, safe obstacles in their habitat to encourage physical movement and give them more places to explore. Avoid sharp or jagged rocks that could injure the tortoise, and ensure the obstacles are low enough for them to navigate comfortably.

b. Mental Stimulation: Problem-Solving and Cognitive Enrichment

Food puzzles and hiding places: One of the simplest and most effective ways to provide mental stimulation is by hiding food in different areas of their enclosure. Tortoises have excellent senses of smell and will naturally "hunt" for food if it is not readily visible. Use puzzle feeders, hide food in piles of leaves or hay, or scatter food in multiple spots to encourage them to search and forage. This simulates the foraging behavior they would naturally exhibit in the wild and keeps their minds sharp.

Digging opportunities: In the wild, leopard tortoises often dig to create shelter, find food, or regulate their body temperature. Providing opportunities for them to dig, such as in a deep substrate of soil, hay, or sand, can be both mentally stimulating and physically beneficial. You can also place food beneath the substrate to further encourage digging behaviors.

Interactive toys: Though tortoises are not as interactive as some other pets, some tortoises enjoy interacting with objects in their environment. A ball or a large, non-toxic rock that they can push or explore might engage their curiosity. However, be mindful that not all tortoises will interact with objects in the same way, so observe how your pet responds and provide safe, non-threatening items for them to explore.

c. Socialization and Interaction

Limited social interaction: While leopard tortoises are solitary in nature, some individuals may benefit from companionship. However, be cautious when keeping more than one tortoise in an enclosure, as territorial behavior or aggression can occur, especially if the tortoises are not familiar with each other. In the wild, they rarely interact unless for mating, so offering a balance of companionship and space is essential.

Human interaction: While leopard tortoises do not crave attention or interaction as much as some other pets, many enjoy gentle handling. They may benefit from calm, positive human interactions such as feeding time or occasionally being moved to different areas within their enclosure. Always handle your tortoise gently and avoid stressing them out with too much handling, as it can disrupt their natural behaviors and cause anxiety.

3. Sensory Enrichment

Leopard tortoises have strong senses of smell and sight, which can be enhanced through sensory stimulation.

a. Smell and Taste

Varied diets: Providing a variety of fresh vegetation will not only encourage natural foraging behaviors but also stimulate their sense of taste. Offering a selection of different plants, flowers, and herbs can keep them interested and provide a richer sensory experience. Experimenting with safe, tortoise-friendly foods like dandelions, clover, and edible flowers will appeal to their natural instincts.

Scent trails: You can create scent trails by dragging fragrant plants or food along the ground of the enclosure. Tortoises will follow the scent trail and engage in natural foraging behaviors to find the source.

b. Sight and Visual Stimulation

New objects: Changing the environment periodically by adding new elements like rocks, plants, or branches can stimulate a tortoise's curiosity. Leopards are naturally inclined to explore their environment, and visual novelty can engage their brain, providing cognitive enrichment.

Outdoor exposure: If possible, allow your tortoise to spend time outdoors where it can experience natural stimuli like sunlight, plants, and wildlife. The ever-changing outdoor environment will engage its senses in a way that an indoor enclosure cannot fully replicate.

Leopard tortoises require both mental and physical stimulation to thrive in captivity. By understanding their natural instincts and providing a stimulating environment that encourages foraging, exploration, and sensory engagement, you can significantly improve their quality of life. Offering a variety of enrichment activities, such as food puzzles, digging opportunities, and environmental changes, can help keep your tortoise healthy, active, and content. In turn, this will result in a happier, healthier pet that enjoys a more natural lifestyle, even within the confines of captivity.

Legal Considerations of Keeping Leopard Tortoises as Pets

Leopard tortoises are a popular exotic pet choice due to their striking appearance and relatively manageable care requirements. However, there are important legal considerations when it comes to owning one of these tortoises, particularly because they are native to sub-Saharan Africa and face specific conservation challenges in the wild. As with any exotic pet, it is crucial for potential tortoise owners to be informed about the regulations surrounding their ownership, as well as the ethical concerns tied to their conservation. Below, we will explore the key legal considerations, including pet ownership regulations and conservation efforts, that must be considered before bringing a leopard tortoise into your home.

1. Regulations on Pet Ownership of Leopard Tortoises

Leopard tortoises, as with many exotic species, are subject to various legal regulations depending on the country or region where they are being kept. These laws are designed to protect the species from over-exploitation, ensure proper care for the animals, and regulate their trade.

a. Laws Governing the Import and Export of Leopard Tortoises

International Trade and CITES: Leopard tortoises are listed under **CITES (the Convention on International Trade in Endangered Species of Wild Fauna and Flora)**. CITES regulates the international trade of certain species to ensure their trade does not threaten their survival in the wild. Leopard tortoises fall under **Appendix II of CITES**, which includes species that are not necessarily threatened with extinction but could become so if trade is not regulated.

This means that any international trade of leopard tortoises must be documented, and permits are required for both exporting and importing them.

Permits and Documentation: If you wish to import or export a leopard tortoise, you must ensure that the tortoise has the necessary permits and documentation that prove it was legally obtained. This includes CITES permits, which verify that the tortoise was bred in captivity or legally sourced. Buying a tortoise without these permits could be illegal and harmful to the species.

Country-Specific Regulations: Different countries have their own regulations regarding the ownership of exotic animals like the leopard tortoise. Some regions may prohibit the importation of leopard tortoises entirely or require specific permits to own them. Always check with local wildlife authorities or animal control agencies to ensure you are compliant with the laws in your area. For example, in certain parts of the United States, there may be state-level restrictions on keeping exotic species or a need for special permits for their care.

b. Legal Requirements for Captive Care and Housing

Enclosure Size and Conditions: While not necessarily part of a national law, many animal control agencies or pet ownership guidelines require that owners of exotic pets, including leopard tortoises, provide adequate living conditions. This includes maintaining a certain size of the enclosure, providing proper temperature and humidity levels, and offering enrichment for the tortoise. Some regions may have laws or regulations that specifically address how tortoises must be housed in captivity to ensure their welfare.

Veterinary Care Requirements: Some countries may require owners of exotic pets to provide access to specialized veterinary care. This ensures that the tortoise's health is regularly monitored, and any diseases or conditions are addressed promptly. For instance, certain species, including the leopard tortoise, are susceptible to respiratory infections, metabolic bone disease, and parasites, which require specialized care.

2. Conservation Efforts and Ethical Concerns

The wild population of leopard tortoises is threatened by habitat loss, illegal trade, and over-exploitation for the pet trade. As a result, conservation efforts and ethical concerns play a critical role in the legal framework for owning these tortoises as pets.

a. Habitat Loss and Threats in the Wild

Natural Habitat Destruction: Leopard tortoises are native to the dry savannahs and grasslands of sub-Saharan Africa, where they play an important role in the ecosystem by grazing on grasses and controlling vegetation growth. Unfortunately, these areas face threats from human activities such as agriculture, urban development, and deforestation. As their natural habitats are destroyed, the tortoises are pushed into smaller and more fragmented regions, reducing their chances of survival.

Impact of Climate Change: Climate change poses another serious threat to leopard tortoises, as it disrupts their natural habitat by altering rainfall patterns, temperatures, and the availability of food sources. Droughts, in particular, can make it difficult for tortoises to find the moisture and plants they need to survive.

b. The Pet Trade and Ethical Concerns

Illegal Wild Capture and Trade: One of the main threats to the leopard tortoise population is the illegal capture and trade of wild-caught individuals for the pet industry. In many regions, these tortoises are poached from the wild and sold on the black market. This illegal trade is not only harmful to the species but also undermines efforts to conserve their natural populations. When purchasing a leopard tortoise, it is crucial to ensure that it was bred in captivity and legally sourced. A tortoise obtained from a reputable breeder is far less likely to be contributing to the depletion of wild populations.

Overpopulation of Captive Leopards: The demand for exotic pets has led to the overbreeding of tortoises, particularly in regions where they are kept as pets. This can lead to overcrowding and unnecessary suffering in captivity. Many leopard tortoises that are bred in captivity face limited space and can suffer from poor living conditions if owners do not provide adequate care or proper veterinary attention.

Ethical Ownership: Ethically, it is important for potential pet owners to consider whether they are prepared to meet the long-term care requirements of a leopard tortoise. Leopard tortoises can live for decades and require specialized care, including proper housing, diet, and medical care. Ethically, owners should ask themselves whether they are equipped to provide a permanent, comfortable, and healthy home for the tortoise for its entire lifespan. In some cases, releasing a captive-bred tortoise into the wild may not be a viable option, as captive tortoises may not have the survival skills needed in their natural habitat.

c. Conservation Breeding Programs

Captive Breeding Programs: To combat the depletion of wild populations, many zoos, wildlife reserves, and research institutions are implementing captive breeding programs to help preserve the species. These programs aim to breed leopard tortoises in controlled environments where they can grow and reproduce without the threat of poaching or habitat destruction. These programs are vital in maintaining the species' population and may provide a source of legally bred tortoises for the pet trade.

Reintroduction Efforts: In some cases, tortoises bred in captivity are reintroduced into the wild as part of conservation efforts. However, successful reintroduction is complex and requires careful planning to ensure that the tortoises are able to survive in their natural habitats. This process often includes habitat restoration, monitoring, and long-term support.

3. How to Ensure Ethical and Legal Ownership

To ensure that you are engaging in responsible and ethical ownership of a leopard tortoise, here are several important steps to take:

a. Purchase from Reputable Sources

Buy captive-bred tortoises: Always purchase a leopard tortoise from a reputable breeder who follows ethical breeding practices. Ensure that the breeder provides you with proper documentation, such as CITES certificates, to verify that the tortoise was bred in captivity and legally sourced.

Check for necessary permits: If you're buying a leopard tortoise from abroad, make sure that both the exporter and importer have obtained the proper CITES permits and other documentation required by your country's wildlife and customs authorities.

b. Understand Your Local Laws

Research local regulations: Before obtaining a leopard tortoise, thoroughly research the laws in your region regarding the ownership, importation, and care of exotic animals. Ensure that you are compliant with all regulations, including those pertaining to enclosure size, veterinary care, and potential permits.

Ensure proper permits for breeding: If you plan to breed leopard tortoises, be sure to obtain any necessary permits for breeding and sale, which may be required in some regions. This is particularly important if you intend to sell or trade the offspring.

c. Support Conservation Initiatives

Contribute to conservation efforts: Consider supporting organizations that are working to protect leopard tortoises and their habitats in the wild. Donating to conservation groups or volunteering for projects related to habitat restoration, anti-poaching efforts, or reintroduction programs can make a significant difference in the survival of the species.

Educate others: Share information with others about the ethical implications of owning exotic pets and encourage responsible pet ownership. Educating others can help reduce the demand for wild-caught tortoises and promote the conservation of species like the leopard tortoise.

The legal considerations and ethical concerns surrounding leopard tortoises as pets are multifaceted. From understanding the regulations governing their importation to considering the conservation challenges they face in the wild, responsible ownership of these tortoises requires awareness and care. By purchasing captive-bred tortoises from ethical sources, adhering to legal requirements, and supporting conservation efforts, owners can contribute to the protection of leopard tortoises while ensuring that their pet thrives in a healthy and enriching environment.

Chapter Ten

Common Myths About Leopard Tortoises

Leopard tortoises are fascinating creatures, often admired for their beautiful patterns and unique behavior. However, like many exotic pets, there are numerous misconceptions and myths about them. These misunderstandings can lead to improper care, mistreatment, and confusion about the responsibilities involved in owning a leopard tortoise. In this section, we will address and debunk some of the most common myths about leopard tortoises, while providing the essential facts you need to know to care for them properly.

1. Myth: Leopard Tortoises Are Low-Maintenance Pets

The Truth

While leopard tortoises might seem like a low-maintenance pet at first glance, they actually require a high level of attention and care to ensure they thrive. As reptiles, they are sensitive to their environment, needing precise temperature, humidity, and lighting conditions.

Enclosure and Habitat: Leopard tortoises need a spacious, well-maintained habitat that mimics their natural environment. Whether kept indoors or outdoors, the enclosure must have the right substrates for digging, ample space for roaming, and safe hiding spots. Indoors, they also need a UVB light source to help them synthesize vitamin D3, which is crucial for calcium absorption.

Dietary Requirements: Leopard tortoises are herbivores, but their diet must be carefully planned to include a variety of grasses, leafy greens, and safe flowers. They are also prone to metabolic bone disease (MBD) if they do not receive enough calcium and UVB exposure.

Long Lifespan: Leopard tortoises can live for several decades, meaning they are a long-term commitment. This is an essential factor to consider before deciding to keep one as a pet.

2. Myth: Leopard Tortoises Can Live in Small Cages

The Truth

Leopard tortoises are large animals and need a spacious environment to roam, explore, and exercise. A small cage or enclosure will not be sufficient for their well-being, and could lead to stress, lethargy, and health problems.

Enclosure Size: A general rule of thumb is that an adult leopard tortoise needs an enclosure that is at least **8 feet by 4 feet**, but larger is always better. A larger space encourages natural behaviors such as grazing, exploring, and even digging, which are vital to their physical and mental health.

Outdoor vs. Indoor Enclosures: Outdoors, leopard tortoises benefit from larger, more natural environments where they can bask in the sun, forage, and dig. Indoor enclosures must still be large enough for them to move around and should have proper lighting, temperature gradients, and substrate that allows for digging.

3. Myth: Leopard Tortoises Can Live in Aquariums or Fish Tanks

The Truth

Aquariums or fish tanks are not appropriate habitats for leopard tortoises. These enclosures are typically too small, lack the proper ventilation, and do not provide enough space for the tortoises to move freely.

Improper Air Circulation: Fish tanks tend to have poor air circulation, which can lead to issues with humidity and temperature regulation. Leopard tortoises need a controlled environment with proper airflow to maintain healthy living conditions.

No Room for Exercise: Tortoises require plenty of space to roam and explore. An aquarium is a confined space that limits their movement and could lead to behavioral issues, such as stress and aggression.

4. Myth: Leopard Tortoises Are Simple to Handle

The Truth

Leopard tortoises are generally not fond of being handled, and excessive handling can lead to stress. While some tortoises may tolerate gentle handling, they are more solitary and independent creatures than many other types of pets.

Handling Stress: Like all reptiles, tortoises can become stressed when handled improperly or too frequently. Handling should be kept to a minimum, limited to necessary tasks such as cleaning the enclosure, moving them to a new location, or during regular health checks.

How to Handle: If you do need to handle a leopard tortoise, ensure that it is done gently and securely. Always support their body properly to avoid causing harm, as their shells and legs can be sensitive to stress. Allow them to roam freely in their space whenever possible.

5. Myth: Leopard Tortoises Can Live on Just Lettuce and Carrots

The Truth

While lettuce and carrots may be an easy go-to for many pet owners, these foods are not ideal for a leopard tortoise's diet. In fact, feeding them a diet consisting primarily of these items can lead to serious nutritional imbalances.

Lack of Nutrition in Lettuce: Most types of lettuce are very low in nutritional value. Iceberg lettuce, for instance, offers little more than water and can cause digestive upset if fed regularly. For a healthy diet, your tortoise needs a wide variety of leafy greens like dandelion greens, collard greens, and mustard greens.

Importance of Grass and Weeds: Leopard tortoises are grazers, and their diet should consist mainly of grasses and weeds. These foods are high in fiber and essential nutrients that promote digestive health and help prevent obesity.

Calcium and Vitamin D3: To avoid metabolic bone disease (MBD), leopard tortoises need a balanced intake of calcium and vitamin D3. Calcium supplements and UVB light exposure are key to ensuring they get enough of these essential nutrients. Avoid feeding them high-oxalate vegetables like spinach or kale, which can interfere with calcium absorption.

6. Myth: Leopard Tortoises Are Low-Social Animals and Don't Need Interaction

The Truth

While leopard tortoises are solitary animals by nature, they still benefit from mental stimulation and occasional interaction. They are not as social as some other reptiles, but they do have individual personalities and can become accustomed to gentle, consistent handling and attention.

Curiosity and Exploration: Leopard tortoises are naturally curious creatures. They enjoy exploring their environment, so providing an enriching enclosure with hiding spots, rocks, and varied terrain is essential for their mental stimulation.

Handling and Bonding: Some leopard tortoises may tolerate light, gentle handling and even recognize their owners over time, associating them with food or positive experiences. However, they are not as interactive as other pets, and it is important to respect their need for space and autonomy.

7. Myth: Leopard Tortoises Are Good for Young Children to Handle

The Truth

While leopard tortoises are generally docile creatures, they are not ideal pets for young children, especially if they are prone to handling them roughly or excessively. Tortoises are not "cuddly" animals, and their slow pace can lead to frustration or unintentional harm when handled improperly.

Potential for Stress: Children may not fully understand the importance of respecting the tortoise's space, and frequent or improper handling can stress out the animal. It's important to supervise any interactions between young children and tortoises to ensure both the child and tortoise are safe and comfortable.

Educational Opportunity: While not ideal for direct interaction, a leopard tortoise can still be a great educational pet for older children. They can learn about reptile care, biology, and conservation by observing and helping with the tortoise's needs.

8. Myth: Leopard Tortoises Are Aggressive and Bite Often

The Truth

Leopard tortoises are not typically aggressive, and while they may occasionally try to defend themselves by retreating into their shells or making a defensive bite, they are not prone to attacking or biting like some other species of animals.

Mild-Mannered Behavior: Most leopard tortoises are gentle and non-aggressive by nature. They may show some mild defensive behavior, especially if they feel threatened or surprised, but these actions are generally more about retreating to safety rather than displaying overt aggression.

Handling and Communication: Tortoises generally communicate through body language, such as withdrawing into their shells when they feel threatened, or pushing away with their front legs if they are disturbed. These behaviors are usually not a sign of aggression, but a natural instinct for self-protection.

9. Myth: Leopard Tortoises Can Live Without Veterinary Care

The Truth

Leopard tortoises, like all pets, require regular veterinary care, particularly from veterinarians who specialize in reptiles. Without proper check-ups, they can suffer from various health issues, including respiratory infections, metabolic bone disease (MBD), and parasites.

Routine Health Checks: It's important to schedule regular veterinary check-ups to monitor the health of your leopard tortoise. These visits can help catch any issues early, such as shell rot, skin infections, or parasitic infestations, before they become severe.

Proper Veterinary Care: A reptile vet can also provide guidance on diet, lighting, and environmental adjustments, ensuring that your tortoise is receiving the care it needs to stay healthy.

Understanding the truths about leopard tortoises is key to providing them with a happy and healthy life. By debunking common myths, you can approach their care with the knowledge and respect they deserve. Remember, leopard tortoises are not low-maintenance or solitary in the ways many myths suggest. They require proper care, a well-designed habitat, a balanced diet, and regular veterinary attention. When given the right environment and attention, leopard tortoises can thrive as rewarding and long-lived companions.

Leopard Tortoise's Role in the Ecosystem

Leopard tortoises are an essential component of their natural ecosystems, particularly in the arid savannas and grasslands of sub-Saharan Africa, where they are native. These tortoises are more than just passive creatures; they actively contribute to the health and balance of their habitats. Understanding their role in the ecosystem is crucial, especially as their populations face threats from habitat destruction, illegal trade, and climate change.

Below is a detailed look at the leopard tortoise's role in nature, its impact on the ecosystem, and why conservation is critical to protecting this species and its habitat.

1. Importance of Leopard Tortoises in Nature

a. Grazers and Seed Dispersers

Leopard tortoises play a vital role in maintaining the balance of their environment through their herbivorous feeding habits. As grazers, they consume a variety of grasses, herbs, and plants, which helps regulate plant growth and prevent overgrowth in the ecosystems they inhabit.

Maintaining Vegetation Balance: By grazing on grasses and other vegetation, leopard tortoises prevent certain plant species from dominating the landscape, thus promoting biodiversity. Without such grazing, some plant species could become invasive, overtake the habitat, and limit the variety of plant life available for other herbivores.

Seed Dispersal: Leopard tortoises contribute to the spread of seeds. As they move around their environment and feed on different plants, they inadvertently swallow seeds, which pass through their digestive systems and are deposited in new locations in their droppings. This dispersal process helps to regenerate plant populations, allowing plant species to spread across a broader area, enhancing biodiversity.

b. Soil Aeration and Habitat Creation

Leopard tortoises are also instrumental in shaping their physical environment, particularly through their digging behavior.

Digging Burrows and Shelters: Tortoises often dig burrows, which they use for shelter and to escape extreme weather conditions such as intense heat. These burrows can also serve as refuges for other animals, such as small mammals, insects, and even other reptiles. These shelters provide protection from predators and offer a stable microhabitat where other species can thrive.

Soil Aeration: When foraging and moving around, leopard tortoises disturb the soil and break up the top layer. This natural aeration helps to improve soil health, allowing water to penetrate deeper into the ground. In areas with dry conditions, such aeration can help water retention in the soil, benefiting both plant life and other animals that rely on the land for food.

c. Role in the Food Chain

Leopard tortoises are part of a complex food web in their ecosystems. While they are herbivores, they also serve as prey for various predators, playing a role in the diet of carnivores.

Predator-Prey Dynamics: As adults, leopard tortoises are not typically preyed upon by many animals due to their size and protective shell. However, their eggs and young hatchlings are vulnerable to predators like birds of prey, foxes, and hyenas. These tortoises, especially in their early life stages, provide an important food source for predators, contributing to the balance of the ecosystem's food chain.

Predators of Insects: In addition to grazing on plants, leopard tortoises sometimes feed on insects or small invertebrates, further contributing to the control of insect populations in their environment.

2. Conservation and Protecting Wild Populations

The leopard tortoise is currently listed as a species of **least concern** by the International Union for Conservation of Nature (IUCN), but this does not mean it is free from threats. As human activity continues to impact wildlife habitats, leopard tortoises face a range of challenges, many of which stem from the destruction of their natural environment and illegal trade practices. Conservation efforts are critical to ensuring the survival of leopard tortoises in the wild.

a. Threats to Leopard Tortoises

Habitat Destruction: Leopard tortoises primarily inhabit dry savannas and grasslands, ecosystems that are under threat from human activities such as agriculture, urbanization, and deforestation. As these areas are cleared for farming or development, tortoises lose both their food sources and their natural shelters, leaving them more vulnerable to predation and extreme environmental conditions.

Illegal Wildlife Trade: Leopard tortoises are often captured from the wild and sold as pets or for use in traditional medicine in some cultures. This illegal trade has a direct impact on wild populations, as it removes individuals from the ecosystem, disrupting breeding cycles and reducing genetic diversity. In addition, wild-caught tortoises often do not survive in captivity, leading to wasted lives and a reduction in the species' overall population.

Climate Change: As climate change leads to more unpredictable weather patterns and higher temperatures, the delicate balance of the tortoises' habitats is disrupted. Increased temperatures and droughts can lead to the loss of vegetation and water sources, which directly affects the tortoise's ability to find food and survive. Extreme heat can also make it difficult for tortoises to regulate their body temperature.

Overgrazing: Overgrazing by domestic livestock can degrade the tortoises' natural habitat. When large herds of cattle or

other grazing animals move through the tortoises'
environment, they can eat the vegetation down to the
ground, leaving little for the tortoises to feed on. This can
lead to food shortages and increased competition for
resources, further threatening the tortoises' survival.

b. Conservation Efforts

Efforts to conserve leopard tortoises are underway in several areas
of sub-Saharan Africa, focusing on habitat preservation, education,
and anti-poaching measures. Conservation programs are essential
for maintaining healthy populations of these tortoises in the wild
and ensuring that future generations of tortoises can thrive in their
natural habitats.

Habitat Protection and Restoration: Many conservation
initiatives focus on protecting existing habitats and
restoring damaged ecosystems. This may involve
preventing illegal land clearing, enforcing protected areas,
and engaging local communities in sustainable land-use
practices. By educating communities about the importance
of leopard tortoises in maintaining ecosystem health, these
programs can reduce human-wildlife conflicts and promote

coexistence.

Captive Breeding and Reintroduction Programs: Some conservation organizations are working with captive breeding programs to help sustain leopard tortoise populations. These programs breed tortoises in controlled environments and, when appropriate, release them back into the wild in suitable habitats. These efforts help boost wild populations, especially in areas where natural populations have declined significantly.

Combating Illegal Trade: Anti-poaching and wildlife trafficking initiatives play a crucial role in reducing the illegal capture and sale of leopard tortoises. These programs involve law enforcement agencies, wildlife rangers, and local communities working together to track and prevent the illegal capture of tortoises, often through surveillance, intelligence gathering, and stricter penalties for those involved in the illegal pet trade.

Research and Monitoring: Ongoing research into the biology, behavior, and ecology of leopard tortoises helps inform conservation strategies. By monitoring populations in the wild, scientists can better understand the needs of these tortoises and identify the specific threats they face. This data is crucial for developing effective conservation programs and ensuring that interventions are appropriately targeted.

3. How You Can Help

As individuals, there are many ways you can contribute to the conservation of leopard tortoises and their habitats:

Support Reputable Conservation Organizations: Donating to or volunteering with wildlife organizations that focus on reptile conservation, such as the Turtle Conservancy or local African wildlife protection groups, can directly support efforts to protect leopard tortoises and their habitats.

Educate Others: Raising awareness about the plight of leopard tortoises and the importance of conserving them is key. By educating others about the consequences of illegal pet trade and habitat destruction, you can help reduce the demand for wild-caught tortoises and encourage more responsible behavior in the pet trade.

Responsible Pet Ownership: If you are a pet owner of a leopard tortoise, ensure that your tortoise was bred in captivity and not taken from the wild. Supporting ethical breeders who follow proper care guidelines can contribute to reducing the pressure on wild populations. Additionally, ensuring proper care and longevity of your pet tortoise can help protect the species overall.

Leopard tortoises play an indispensable role in their ecosystems, contributing to plant diversity, soil health, and the food chain. However, their survival is under threat from various factors, including habitat destruction, illegal trade, and climate change. Protecting wild populations of leopard tortoises requires ongoing conservation efforts, habitat restoration, and education. By supporting these efforts and practicing responsible pet ownership, we can help ensure that leopard tortoises continue to play their vital role in nature for generations to come.

Chapter Eleven

Troubleshooting Common Issues in Leopard Tortoise Care

Leopard tortoises are generally hardy animals, but like all pets, they can experience health or behavioral issues if their environment, diet, or care routines are not optimal. As a pet owner, it's essential to be proactive and knowledgeable about common problems so that you can troubleshoot effectively and ensure your tortoise stays healthy and comfortable. Below is a detailed guide to help you troubleshoot some of the most common issues faced by leopard tortoise owners.

1. Habitat Issues

a. Inadequate Temperature or Humidity

Leopard tortoises are ectothermic animals, meaning they rely on external heat sources to regulate their body temperature. If their environment does not have the correct temperature or humidity levels, it can lead to health problems.

Signs: Lethargy, lack of appetite, frequent hiding, respiratory issues, or abnormal behavior like excessive drinking or urinating.

Troubleshooting:

Temperature: Leopard tortoises need a **warm basking spot** with temperatures around **95-100°F (35-37°C)** and a **cooler area** of **75-85°F (24-29°C)**. The **nighttime temperature** should not drop below **65°F (18°C)**.

Use a **basking lamp** or **ceramic heat emitter** for heat. If using a basking lamp, ensure that it's placed high enough to avoid overheating the tortoise.

Humidity: The humidity level should be around **40-60%**, with higher humidity levels (up to 80%) in the nighttime to prevent dehydration. You can achieve this by spraying the enclosure with water, adding a humidifier, or using a moist substrate like coconut coir. Regularly monitor with a **hygrometer** to ensure levels are stable.

Solution: Install a **thermostat** or a **digital thermometer** and **humidity gauge** to maintain proper environmental control. Adjust the positioning of heat lamps, ventilation, or humidity sources as necessary.

b. Incorrect Lighting (UVB Issues)

UVB light is essential for leopard tortoises to produce vitamin D3, which helps them metabolize calcium. Without it, they may develop **metabolic bone disease (MBD)** or other bone-related issues.

Signs: Soft or deformed shell, abnormal growth, lethargy, muscle weakness, difficulty walking, or a lack of appetite.

Troubleshooting:

UVB Lighting: Ensure you have a **UVB bulb** (UVA/UVB combined, designed for reptiles) that provides **290-320 nm of UVB radiation**. Replace the bulb every 6-12 months, even if it still emits visible light, as the UVB output decreases over time.

Position the UVB light about **6-12 inches above the tortoise**, ensuring they receive exposure for **12-14 hours a day**. If your tortoise spends significant time indoors, invest in a **UVB bulb** that is specifically designed for reptile use and make sure it provides the correct intensity.

Outdoor Tortoises: If you house your tortoise outside, make sure they have access to **direct sunlight** for at least 2-4 hours a day. A shaded area can also be important for temperature regulation.

2. Diet-Related Issues

a. Improper Diet and Obesity

Feeding a leopard tortoise an imbalanced or inappropriate diet can lead to health problems like obesity, nutritional deficiencies, or gastrointestinal issues.

Signs: Weight gain, lethargy, difficulty moving, shell deformities, or digestive issues (e.g., diarrhea or constipation).

Troubleshooting:

- **Appropriate Diet**: Leopard tortoises are herbivores and require a **high-fiber, low-protein diet**. Offer a variety of **grass hay, dark leafy greens** (e.g., dandelion greens, collard greens), and **edible flowers**. Limit high-protein foods like lettuce, spinach, or cabbage, as these can contribute to digestive or shell issues.

- **Calcium and Vitamin D**: Ensure they receive adequate calcium (about 1 part calcium to 10 parts phosphorus) and vitamin D3, especially if they are housed indoors. Use a calcium supplement that contains **no phosphorus** and a multivitamin once a week.

- **Portion Control**: Provide enough food to last the tortoise the day, but avoid overfeeding. Obesity can strain their limbs, reduce mobility, and affect their overall health.

Solution: Evaluate the tortoise's body condition regularly. If it's gaining weight excessively, reduce the portions of high-calcium greens and ensure they are eating a balanced diet that mimics their natural feeding patterns.

b. Dehydration

Dehydration can occur if a tortoise is not consuming enough water or is kept in an environment that is too dry.

Signs: Sunken eyes, dry or flaky skin, lethargy, refusal to eat, or excessive urination.

Troubleshooting:

Hydration: Offer fresh water every day in a shallow dish. Ensure the dish is low enough for the tortoise to drink from easily, but deep enough to avoid tipping over.

Bathing: Soak your tortoise in lukewarm water for **10-15 minutes** every few days to help with hydration. This is particularly important for tortoises that seem to refuse drinking or show signs of dehydration.

Humidity Levels: If your tortoise is housed indoors, ensure that humidity levels are sufficient. Mist the enclosure daily or provide a moist substrate to encourage natural moisture absorption through the skin.

Solution: Always monitor hydration closely, especially in young or elderly tortoises, as they are more prone to dehydration. Adjust the humidity and provide plenty of water sources in their habitat.

3. Behavioral Issues

a. Lethargy or Lack of Appetite

If your leopard tortoise is not eating or seems unusually lethargic, it may be a sign that something is wrong with its environment or health.

> **Signs**: Sleeping more than usual, refusing food, not moving around, or staying hidden for extended periods.

> **Troubleshooting**:

> > **Environmental Stress**: Check if temperature, humidity, and lighting are within the recommended ranges. Make sure your tortoise has access to proper basking areas and areas of shade to regulate their body temperature.

> > **Diet**: Ensure you are offering a balanced, varied diet of fresh, high-fiber plants and grasses. Avoid offering the same food every day, as variety is important for their digestion and appetite.

Illness: If environmental conditions are correct and
they are still not eating, it could indicate an illness,
such as a respiratory infection or parasites. In this
case, seek veterinary advice.

Solution: Ensure that the environment is stable and
appropriate. If the problem persists, consult with a
veterinarian who specializes in reptiles for a health checkup
and further diagnosis.

b. Aggressive Behavior

Leopard tortoises are generally calm and gentle, but in some cases,
they may display aggressive behavior, especially during mating
season or if they feel threatened.

Signs: Biting, head-bobbing, pushing against objects or other
animals, or excessive territorial behavior.

Troubleshooting:

Stressors: Determine if there are stressors in the
environment, such as overcrowding, improper
handling, or other pets in the vicinity. If you house

more than one tortoise, ensure they have sufficient space to avoid territorial disputes.

Breeding Behavior: During breeding season, males can become more aggressive, often engaging in head-bobbing or trying to mount females. This is a natural behavior but can sometimes be distressing.

Habitat Enrichment: Provide enrichment items such as hides, logs, or rocks that allow the tortoises to establish territories or create safe spaces where they can retreat when feeling stressed.

Solution: If aggression persists, provide separate enclosures for individual tortoises or create more hiding spots and territorial boundaries to reduce confrontations.

4. Shell Problems

a. Shell Rot

Shell rot is a fungal or bacterial infection that can cause damage to the tortoise's shell, leading to soft spots or lesions.

Signs: Soft or discolored patches on the shell, foul odor, visible discharge from affected areas.

Troubleshooting:

- **Cleanliness**: Maintain a clean and dry environment for your tortoise. Regularly remove waste from their enclosure and change bedding to avoid the growth of bacteria or fungus.
- **Proper Drying**: Ensure the shell is properly dried after any soaking or bathing. Wet conditions can exacerbate shell rot.
- **Veterinary Care**: If shell rot is suspected, consult a veterinarian immediately. Treatment may include cleaning the affected area, applying antiseptics, and possibly administering antibiotics or antifungal medications.
- **Solution**: Regularly check the shell for signs of damage or infection. Keep their habitat clean, dry, and well-ventilated to prevent fungal and bacterial growth.

By being proactive and observant, you can easily troubleshoot many common issues that arise in the care of leopard tortoises. Regular monitoring of their environment, diet, and behavior is crucial for preventing problems before they escalate. When issues do arise, addressing them quickly and effectively will ensure your tortoise leads a healthy, happy life. If problems persist or you're unsure about diagnosis or treatment, always consult with a reptile veterinarian to get expert advice and care.

25 Frequently Asked Questions (FAQs) About Leopard Tortoises

Leopard tortoises are popular pets due to their fascinating appearance and relatively easy care needs. However, as with any pet, owning a leopard tortoise comes with unique responsibilities. Below is a list of 25 frequently asked questions (FAQs) about leopard tortoises, along with detailed explanations to help you understand how to care for them.

1. What is a leopard tortoise?

A **leopard tortoise** (Stigmochelys pardalis) is a large species of tortoise native to Africa, known for its striking yellow and black patterned shell. They are one of the largest tortoises found in Africa and are herbivores, feeding mainly on grasses and plants. They are prized in the pet trade for their unique appearance.

2. How long do leopard tortoises live?

Leopard tortoises have a long lifespan, often living between **50-100 years** in the wild or captivity, depending on their care and environment. With proper care, they can live well over 50 years in captivity.

3. What is the natural habitat of the leopard tortoise?

In the wild, leopard tortoises are typically found in **savannas, grasslands,** and **semi-arid regions** across sub-Saharan Africa. They prefer areas with moderate temperatures, dry conditions, and some access to water sources. Their natural habitat provides plenty of **grasses** and **low-lying plants** for food.

4. How big do leopard tortoises get?

Leopard tortoises are relatively large. Adult males typically reach **12-18 inches (30-45 cm)** in length, while females are usually **16-24 inches (40-60 cm)**. They can weigh anywhere from **15 to 50 pounds (7-23 kg)**, depending on their size and diet.

5. How do I set up the ideal enclosure for a leopard tortoise?

The ideal enclosure for a leopard tortoise depends on whether it will be housed indoors or outdoors:

Indoor Enclosure: A large **tank or terrarium** (at least **4 feet by 2 feet**) with ample space for the tortoise to move freely. Use a **substrate** like coconut coir, a **basking spot** with a temperature of **95-100°F (35-37°C)**, and a **cooler area** of **75-85°F (24-29°C)**. Provide UVB lighting for **12-14 hours a day**.

Outdoor Enclosure: A **secure, fenced area** (at least **10 feet by 10 feet**) with access to sunlight, shade, and a variety of grasses. Ensure there are no escape routes, as leopard tortoises can climb and dig.

6. What temperature should I maintain for my leopard tortoise?

Leopard tortoises require a **basking temperature of 95-100°F (35-37°C)** during the day, with a cooler area of around **75-85°F (24-29°C)**. At night, the temperature should not drop below **65°F (18°C)**. A **thermostat** and a **digital thermometer** are important tools to monitor temperatures effectively.

7. How do I ensure my leopard tortoise gets enough UVB light?

UVB light is crucial for **vitamin D3 synthesis** and calcium absorption. To provide adequate UVB, use a **UVB fluorescent bulb** specifically designed for reptiles. The bulb should be placed **6-12 inches** above the tortoise. Change the UVB bulb every **6-12 months**, as its UV output diminishes over time, even if the light still works.

8. How often should I feed my leopard tortoise?

Leopard tortoises should be fed daily. They are **herbivores**, and their diet should consist of **grasses, leafy greens**, and **edible flowers**. Offer food that is fresh and varied to keep them healthy. Young tortoises may eat more frequently, while adults can be fed in larger portions once a day.

9. What should I feed my leopard tortoise?

Leopard tortoises require a **high-fiber, low-protein** diet. Offer a variety of:

> **Grasses** (such as timothy hay)
> **Leafy greens** (e.g., collard greens, dandelion greens, kale)
> **Edible flowers** (hibiscus, clover)

Weeds (plantain, chickweed)

Avoid feeding **fruits, lettuce,** or **high-protein foods** such as
cabbage, as these can cause digestive issues and calcium
imbalance.

10. How much should I feed my leopard tortoise?

Provide enough food for your tortoise to eat throughout the day,
but avoid overfeeding. Offer a variety of food that is **about the
size of their shell** in daily servings. It's important to ensure that
they finish their food within the day to avoid rotting and attracting
pests.

11. How often should I bathe my leopard tortoise?

Bathing is important for hydration, especially if your tortoise is not
drinking enough water. Soak your tortoise in **lukewarm water** for
10-15 minutes once or twice a week. For tortoises in dry
environments, more frequent soaking may be necessary.

12. How do I handle a leopard tortoise?

When handling a leopard tortoise, always **support its body** to avoid strain on its legs or shell. Use both hands to lift it gently by the sides of its body or under its shell. Avoid picking it up by its legs or tail. Never handle your tortoise excessively, as it can cause stress.

13. Can leopard tortoises live with other reptiles or pets?

Leopard tortoises are generally peaceful but should be kept separately from other pets or reptiles. They may become stressed or territorial if housed with other animals. If you house multiple tortoises, ensure they have **enough space** to avoid territorial aggression.

14. How do I know if my leopard tortoise is sick?

Signs of illness in a leopard tortoise may include:

- **Lethargy or lack of appetite**
- **Abnormal shell appearance** (soft or discolored patches)
- **Wheezing or discharge from the nose** (signs of respiratory infection)
- **Swollen or watery eyes**

If you notice any of these signs, consult a **veterinarian** who specializes in reptiles.

15. What is metabolic bone disease (MBD)?

Metabolic bone disease (MBD) is a condition caused by a lack of **calcium**, **vitamin D3**, or an **imbalanced diet**. It leads to soft, deformed shells, weak bones, and difficulty moving. MBD is preventable with proper diet and UVB lighting. If you suspect MBD, consult a veterinarian for treatment.

16. How do I treat shell rot in leopard tortoises?

Shell rot is typically caused by **bacteria or fungi** and can cause discoloration, foul odor, and soft spots on the shell. If you notice these symptoms, take your tortoise to a reptile vet for treatment. Treatment may involve cleaning the affected areas, applying antiseptic, and using antibiotics or antifungals.

17. How do I clean my leopard tortoise's enclosure?

Regular cleaning is essential for a healthy environment. Remove waste daily, replace wet or soiled bedding, and clean the enclosure weekly using reptile-safe cleaners. Wash all food and water dishes regularly, and ensure any decorations or accessories are cleaned to avoid bacterial growth.

18. Can leopard tortoises live outside year-round?

Leopard tortoises can live outside in warmer climates with proper shelter and security. However, they should be brought indoors or provided with **a heated indoor shelter** during winter months if temperatures fall below **65°F (18°C)**. Ensure the enclosure is **secure** to prevent escapes.

19. What is the lifespan of a captive leopard tortoise?

Leopard tortoises in captivity can live between **50 and 100 years** with proper care. Their lifespan depends on environmental conditions, diet, and healthcare.

20. How do I prevent my leopard tortoise from escaping?

Leopard tortoises are skilled diggers and climbers. To prevent escapes:

Use **secure fencing** that is at least **2 feet high**.

Bury the bottom of the fence about 6 inches below ground to prevent digging.

Ensure no gaps or openings that could allow your tortoise to climb over or slip through.

21. Do leopard tortoises need a companion?

Leopard tortoises do not require companionship and can live happily on their own. However, if you choose to keep multiple tortoises, make sure there is plenty of space for each tortoise to have its own territory to avoid aggression and stress.

22. Can I breed leopard tortoises in captivity?

Yes, leopard tortoises can breed in captivity if the proper conditions are met. This includes a **properly sexed pair**, a large enclosure, and an appropriate breeding season. Female tortoises may lay eggs even without a male, but the eggs will not hatch.

23. How do I care for baby leopard tortoises?

Baby leopard tortoises require a **warm** and **humid** environment. Keep them in an enclosure with proper UVB lighting, **warm basking areas**, and appropriate food (mainly grasses and greens).

Provide **regular hydration** and frequent soaking to promote healthy growth.

24. How do I keep my leopard tortoise healthy?

To keep your leopard tortoise healthy:

Provide a **balanced diet** with appropriate nutrients.

Ensure a **proper habitat** with appropriate temperatures, humidity, and UVB lighting.

Take your tortoise for **regular vet check-ups**.

Avoid overcrowding, stress, and improper handling.

25. Are leopard tortoises endangered?

Leopard tortoises are not currently considered endangered, but they face threats in the wild due to **habitat loss, illegal pet trade**, and **over-exploitation**. Conservation efforts are in place to protect wild populations. Ethical ownership and responsible breeding are important in supporting their long-term survival.

These FAQs address the most common concerns and queries about leopard tortoises, helping potential pet owners make informed decisions and providing care guidelines to ensure a happy and healthy life for their tortoises.